OPINIONS

ON

INTERESTING SUBJECTS

OF

PUBLIC LAW AND COMMERCIAL POLICY;

ARISING FROM

AMERICAN INDEPENDENCE.

OPINIONS

ON

INTERESTING SUBJECTS

OF

PUBLIC LAW AND COMMERCIAL POLICY;

ARISING FROM

AMERICAN INDEPENDENCE.

§ 1. The Question answered—Whether the Citizens of the United States are considered by the Law of England as Aliens; what Privileges are they entitled to within the Kingdom; what Rights can they claim in the remaining Colonies of Britain.

§ 2. The Regulations for opening the American Trade considered; Faults found; and Amendments proposed: How the late Proclamations affect the United States discussed: Objections pointed out; and Alterations suggested.

§ 2. How far the British West Indies were injured by the late Proclamations fully investigated; the Amount of their Wants discovered; Modes of Supply shewn: And the Policy of admitting the American Vessels into their Ports amply argued.

§ 3. An Enquiry how far a Commercial Treaty with the United States is necessary, or would be advantageous: What the Laws of England have already provided on this Subject; and the fundamental Laws of the United States compared with them.

BY GEORGE CHALMERS,

AUTHOR OF

POLITICAL ANNALS OF THE REVOLTED COLONIES,

AND OF

AN ESTIMATE OF THE COMPARATIVE STRENGTH OF BRITAIN.

LONDON:

Printed for J. DEBRETT, opposite Burlington-House, Piccadilly. 1784.

First Published 1784

Reprinted 1970

I UNDERSTAND not the World fo little as not to know, that he that will faithfully ferve his Country, muft be content to pafs through good report and evil report: Neither regard I which I meet with: TRUTH I AM SURE AT LAST WILL VINDICATE ITSELF, and BE FOUND BY MY COUNTRYMEN, faid

SIR JOSHUA CHILD.

LIBRARY OF CONGRESS CATALOG CARD NUMBER:
70-124784

PRINTED IN THE UNITED STATES OF AMERICA

O P I N I O N S

ON

INTERESTING SUBJECTS

OF

PUBLIC LAW and COMMERCIAL POLICY;

ARISING FROM

AMERICAN INDEPENDENCE.

THE acknowledgment of the Independence of the United States of America was certainly an event of confiderable confequence to Great-Britain. To be freed from foreign war is always an object, which cannot be purchafed at too high a price, while the national honour is preferved. The enjoyment of domeftic tranquility, with all its pleafures and its benefits, is a bleffing of ftill higher value, which cannot be too much prized ; and ought therefore to be preferved by almoft any facrifice.

When the Provisional Articles closed the American controversy, which having endured for years, had embittered private enjoyment and disturbed public repose, an unusual calm ensued. But, in a nation, where interest is always active and faction is often malicious; where many communicate their thoughts on state transactions, because every one has a right to do so; the long continuance of quiet is more to be desired, than reasonably to be hoped for.

The situation, as new as it is obscure, wherein the peace had placed Great Britain and the United States, gave rise to many difficult questions of public law and commercial policy. The attention of the world was again roused, by successive publications; which propagated very different opinions and proposed very dissimilar measures. Amid these anxieties many ask for intelligence; some to gratify prepossession; a few to exalt avarice: But, he who, in order to allay that solicitude, by endeavouring to instruct himself before he presumes to offer instruction to others, may claim at least a patient perusal, while he discharges the duty, which he owes to a public, inquisitive and liberal. The author of the following sheets in this spirit submits his humble sentiments on topicks, whereon the well-meaning and intelligent have thought very variously, with that freedom which belongs to one, who is conscious of good intentions without interest, and with that plainness of language, which

is

is more ftudious of perfpicuity than ambitious of ornament.

§ 1. It is of importance furely to know, prior to any ftable regulation of the American trade, by the legiflature, whether the citizens of the American States are now confidered by our laws as fubjects, or as aliens. Certainty in jurifprudence is doubt-lefs the beft preventive of difputes. Yet, is there little faid on a queftion, fo interefting to many hearts, in the treaty, which acknowledged the in-dependence of the United States. To point out however what might have been provided on this difficult fubject, either by previous act of Parliament, or by fubfequent ftipulation, would only carry us into a thorny path, leading to a field, unfruitful of amufement or inftruction. To examine the face of things as they are is as much the bufinefs of Statefmen, as it is the duty of legiflators to look back only with a regard to the profpect.

The treaty, it muft be however allowed, is ex-plicit enough, as to the political affociations, that compofe THE STATES, which are acknowledged to be free and independent; but it is altogether filent as to THE INDIVIDUALS, who formed thofe celebrated confederations: It admits the thirteen focieties, in their affociated capacity, to be fovereign, by relinquifhing all claim of government over them : But, it does not explicitly renounce the allegiance of the colonifts, who, at the epoch of the peace, were ftill Britifh fubjects, in contempla-tion of Britifh law. For, it does not declare, that

B 2

the

the citizens of the United States shall be deemed aliens in future : And, it as little makes any exception of those faithful subjects ; who, having refused to renounce their allegiance, were denominated *Nonjurors*, by the American code ; and who, having never done any act inconsistent with their fidelity to the Crown, merited at least by their hazards the accustomed stipulation, that they might dispose of their property, without hindrance, and afterwards retire, without further persecution.

The mere act of residence, within the limits assigned to the United States, might have been considered as a misfortune, but it could not surely have been deemed an offence. To submit to a force which they could not resist ; to pay treble taxes that they could not refuse ; are regarded as crimes by no social system, except by the new-fangled laws of South Carolina alone *. Happily different is our constitution in this respect : With the united voice of reason and humanity it declares : " That if enemies or rebels come with a superior force and exact contributions, submission is not so much criminal as prudent, to prevent a public evil of greater magnitude †."

The American Nonjurors having been born within the king's dominions, were by that circumstance

---

* The Jacksonborough Assembly of 1782 excluded from the right of citizenship all those, who having made a temporary submission to the British army, were denominated *protection-men.*

† Forster's Crown Law, 8vo. edit. p. 217.

ftance alone conftituted freemen of this realm : By
their birth within the allegiance of the Crown they
acquired a variety of rights, which by our lawyers
are emphatically ftyled their *birth-rights*; and which
can never be forfeited, except by their own mif-
behaviour, and can never be taken away, but by
the will of their fellow-citizens, expreffed by act of
Parliament. An alien cannot be admitted a freeman of this kingdom without the confent of the community, by an act of naturalization : neither can
an innocent freeman be disfranchifed, except by
the conjoint voice of the nation. And the reafon
of both thofe rules may be found in the original
compact itfelf; which provided, that no one fhould
be admitted a contracting party, without the confent of the whole ; which equally declared, that a
contracting party fhould not be deprived of the advantages of the compact, while he faithfully performed his original ftipulations. What ought thus
to be the fundamental principle of every Government is exprefsly recognized by THE GREAT
CHARTER of England; whofe language can no
more become obfolete, than its provifions in favour
of the rights of human nature can ceafe to operate.
No freeman, fays the boaft of Britain, *fhall be feized,
or imprifoned, or outlawed, or any way deftroyed, except by the legal judgment of his peers, or by the law
of the land.* But to expel a meritorious body of
men from the fociety whereof they had once been
members is at once to outlaw and deftroy them.
The American Loyalifts faithfully performed their
                                                      original

original ſtipulations; it was their misfortune and their only crime, that after they had riſqued and loſt more than common ſubjeſts, the community did not, in return, yield them merited protection.

If the moſt inſignificant ſubjeſt cannot then be deprived of the moſt trivial privilege, without the moſt poſitive law, we may confidently infer, that a deſerving claſs of ſubjeſts cannot be bereaved of every ſocial right, by mere implication. Years have ſcarcely paſſed away, ſince wiſe men and profound lawyers differed in opinion, whether the aſt of Parliament, empowering the Crown to make peace or a truce, with the revolted Colonies, enabled the Miniſters of the Crown to acknowledge the Independence of the United States. Whatever foundation there might have been for that unhappy difference, the ſubſequent recognition of the Legiſlature has removed every future doubt. Yet, had a power been poſitively given to renounce the allegiance of thoſe colonial ſubjeſts, who, in oppoſition to violence and even to negleſt, remained unalterably attached to the Britiſh Government, that power has not been by the Treaty of Peace in any manner executed; as we may learn from its ſilence, where it ought to have ſpoken in the moſt audible tone. In confirmation of the general inference, that the before-mentioned loyal perſons, who, at the epoch of the peace, remained within the limits of the United States, are ſtill conſidered as ſubjeſts by our laws, judicial authorities might

might be quoted, if it were thought neceſſary to cite the deciſions of judges for the eſtabliſhment of doctrines; which, having been interwoven into our conſtitution, are taught us in our youth and are imprinted on our hearts.

It is neverthelefs a very different conſideration, with refpect to thoſe Coloniſts; who having at-chieved the late revolution, by their efforts, now form, by their reſidence, the citizens of the United States. Rights may be undoubtedly forfeited, though privileges cannot be arbitrarily taken away. A man's crimes, or even miſconduct, may deprive him of thoſe immunities, which he might have claimed from birth, or derived from an act of the Legiſlature: He may be outlawed by the ſentence of a court of juſtice, or he may be baniſhed by the united ſuffrages of his countrymen. The Ame-rican citizens, who voluntarily abjured their So-vereign, avowed their deſign to relinquiſh the cha-racter of ſubjects: The American citizens, who ſwore allegiance to the Government of their own choice, thereby declared their election, that they would be no longer connected with a State, which had mortified their prejudices rather than bereaved them of rights: And by that conduct and by thoſe offences the revolted Coloniſts forfeited to the law all that the law had ever conferred. The Ame-rican Treaty however acknowledged that avowal: The recognition of Parliament legalized that elec-tion. But, whether that act of the Britiſh Govern-ment, or that act of the Britiſh Legiſlature, ought

to

to be conſtrued as a relinquiſhment of their obedience, or as a pardon of their faults, is a problem,
which, at this day, does not merit a formal ſolu-
tion.

The law of England (as we all know) hath
divided the reſidents within the Britiſh dominions
into two claſſes; 1ſtly, into that of ſubjeɛts; 2dly,
into that of aliens, who are ſubdivided into a body
denominated denizens; a name, which implies,
that they had once been aliens, but had been admitted by their denization, to ſome of the privileges of ſubjeɛts.

But the law of England knows nothing aſſuredly
of a *real* ſubjeɛt, or *unreal* ſubjeɛt; to affirm of a
perſon, that he is more a ſubjeɛt or leſs a ſubjeɛt is to
ſpeak neither good Engliſh, nor ſound law; ſince
the term ſubjeɛt does not admit of degrees: And
every one muſt conſequently be either a ſubjeɛt to
all intents, or to no intent. To admit novelties
into our language is almoſt as dangerous, as it is
to allow innovations in our law. The unmeaning
epithet *real* was prefixed in the Treaty * to the well-
known terms *Britiſh ſubjeɛts*, with deſign to dif-
tinguiſh thoſe Britiſh ſubjeɛts, who, having been
born without the United States, never permanently
reſided

* The American negotiators have at length explained to
the world the import of the perplexing expreſſions *real* Britiſh
ſubjeɛts, by their letter to the Congreſs, dated the 18th of
July 1783, and publiſhed in the Pennſylvania Independent
Gazette of the 24th of April, 1784: " The Britiſh Miniſters, ſay the negotiators, were unwilling to make uſe of
any

resided within them, from those British subjects, who, having fixedly dwelt within the revolted Colonies, risqued their persons, and sacrificed their all at the shrine of their attachments to the British Government. A narcotick was to be found, it seems, to prevent those meritorious subjects from feeling their wounds, though they had been already wounded beyond cure. But, on whatever motive the British negotiators acted, the American negotiators inserted those unusual expressions into the Treaty, in order to gain the virtual acknowledgment of the British Government, that the British Colonies had always been independent, or at least intitled to Independence: in making that virtual acknowledgment the British Government in some measure admitted, that there had existed *American* subjects and *British* subjects; that the American loyalists, having been American subjects, had incurred confiscation, because, in their active adherence to the British Government, they had violated their allegiance to the United States. The pretension and the admission were both equally irrational and illegal. Yet, by that signal transaction both parties affirmed,

C

any terms that might give uneasiness to the *Refugee Tories*, and the terms *real British subjects* were well understood and ascertained, not to mean, or comprehend *American Refugees*: and it was only a more delicate mode of excluding the *Refugees*, and making a proper distinction between them and the subjects of Britain, *whose only particular interest in America* consisted *in holding lands and property*." And thus have we ascertained who are, and who are not, *real British subjects*.

affirmed, that the citizens of the United States were to be regarded in future as aliens.

The American citizens can therefore, by no mode of fpeech, or by any principle of law, be deemed Britifh fubjeacts; unlefs thofe affociations of mankind are fubjeacts, who owe no allegiance to the Britifh Crown, or any obedience to the Britifh Government; that allegiance, which is faid to include all the engagements owing from fubject to Sovereign ; that obedience, which is ftyled emphatically the very effence of law. But, the King of Great-Britain has formally relinquifhed all claim of fovereignty over the United States and all pretence of government over the American citizens : And the Parliament, by recognizing the act of renunciation, virtually expreffed the affent of the community to the expulfion of the American citizens from the focial compact, which binds every member of the Britifh State together. The citizens of the United States are not certainly denizens, becaufe they can fhew no letters of denization, which indeed would prove, that they had therefore been aliens. Now, he who is neither a fubject, nor a denizen, is deemed by the law of England an alien.

Were we to turn over only a few pages of hiftory, the faithful handmaid of jurifprudence, we might difcover illuflrations of the foregoing reafonings, though we fhould probably find no precedent of a people, who continued Englifh fubjeacts, after the Englifh Government had renounced

their

their obedience. The ancient annals of Scotland will furnish striking examples. When Edward I. acquired by his policy from the meanness of Baliol more than by his power from the submission of the nobles, the virtual sovereignty, though not the direct dominion of Scotland, the Scots became by that signal event the fellow subjects of Englishmen: When Scotland, in her turn regained, by the gallantry or prudence of Bruce, her ancient independence, the Scots immediately became aliens to their too powerful neighbours: Yet, the English did not formally renounce the government of a nation, whose obedience they were unable to enforce. And the Scots continued aliens even after the fortunate accession of James i. to the throne of England. Those Scotsmen alone, who were born after that epoch, were considered as fellow subjects of Englishmen, till a much happier event united inseparably the two people together.

If from our island we turn our inquiries to the neighbouring continent, we shall find, that Normandy and Aquitain, Tournay and Calais, were unfortunately once possessed by the monarchs of England. During that said period, of foreign expeditions and domestic penury; the residents of each of those countries enjoyed all the privileges of subjects. When each however became successively separated from this realm, by the imbecilities of folly co-operating with the efforts of ambition, the inhabitants of all those foreign dominions became, in their turn, aliens to the

C 2   Crown.

Crown. France too was conquered in an evil hour by England, during the glorious yet miserable days of our Edwards   The French became by that unfalutary meafure the fellow fubjects of Englifhmen. And to this hour the Britifh fovereign enjoys the flattering though unproductive title of King of France: Yet, the French for ages have not been confidered as Britifh fubjects; fince they certainly owe no allegiance to the Britifh Crown, or yield any fubmiffion to the Britifh Government. The fame ftroke of fortune, either adverfe or happy, which deprived the refidents of all thofe provinces and towns of the protection of one common Sovereign, broke afunder the bands of allegiance, that formed the connection between them: For, the Englifh Government being either renounced, or withdrawn, the people continued no longer fubjects than their obedience could be afked and enjoined.

Of the truth of the foregoing reafoning the ceffion of Surinam by Charles II. to the Dutch furnifhes a direct proof. By the treaty of Breda it was agreed, " That both parties fhould retain with *plenary right of fovereignty, propriety, and poffeffion,* all fuch lands, iflands, and colonies, as either had theretofore gotten, or retained from the other."— Thefe expreffions are general ; yet, indefinite as they are, they were deemed fufficiently energetic to transfer the allegiance of the Englifh colonifts to the States-General and the allegiance of the Dutch colonifts at New-York to the Englifh Crown

Crown. The Englifh inhabitants of Surinam were thenceforth confidered, by the ableft ftatefmen of both countries, as fo exclufively the fubjects of the United Netherlands, that the King of England could not even interpofe as mediator between their new fovereigns * and them. In this manner were the expreffions *plenary right of fovereignty* conftrued to have converted colonifts, who had once been fubjects, into aliens, who could no longer claim the privileges or protection of the parent ftate. And from this decifive precedent we may infer, that there was no neceffity to infert, in the American Treaty, a claufe, renouncing the allegiance of the colonifts, fince the fovereignty of the country being relinquifhed and the government withdrawn, it could anfwer no good purpofe to retain the faith and fubmiffion of the people.

It feems thus impoffible to repel thofe general inferences and that legal conclufion, by the moft liberal conftruction, which has been ever made of the various ftatutes of naturalization from the days of Edward I. to the prefent. The well known law † of that celebrated conqueror appears to have received an explanation much larger than the narrownefs of the words would at firft fight juftify. The capacity to inherit, which by them were given to the children, " Whofe *father* and
mother

* MSS. Memorial of John De Witt, with the anfwer thereto.

† 25 Ed. III. Stat. 2. " Of thofe that be born beyond the Sea."

mother were at the faith of the King, and who should be born without the ligeance of the Crown," has been enlarged by judges, who wished to contract the disabilities of aliens, into an act of naturalization *. For, it has been decided, " That though an English merchant marry a *foreigner* and has issue by her born beyond the seas, that issue is a natural born subject; yet, if an English woman go beyond seas and marry an alien, who have issue born beyond the sea, *that issue are aliens*."

Such was the law prior to the reign of Anne; though an act † of Parliament was passed soon after the Restoration, in favour of a meritorious class of men, the children of those ardent loyalists, who had followed the fortunes of Charles II. into exile. It was owing more perhaps to momentary passion than to any well-weighed policy, that the statute of Anne ‡ was passed—" for naturalizing foreign Protestants." A collateral clause of this act declared, " That the children of natural born subjects, born out of the ligeance of the Crown, shall be deemed natural born subjects of this kingdom." And the act recited, as the moving principle of the legislature, " That the encrease of people is the means of advancing the wealth and strength of a nation." General positions in political

* Molloy Dejure Marit. Book iii, of Aliens.
† 29 Cha. II. chap. 6.
‡ 7 Ann. chap. 5.

tical œconomy always lead to mischievous error.
The Parliament discovered ere long, that they had
applied the nostrum of a quack in a case, where
they should have administered the medicine of a
physician. And it became apparent at least to the
wise, that giving employment to the idle is
the only mode of promoting the encrease of
the people, and of advancing the wealth and
strength of a nation; while the inviting of
foreigners into a country, whose inhabitants are
not fully employed, is at once to starve the poor
and beggar the rich. Owing to these causes probably the clause of the statute of Anne, which had
naturalized all foreign Protestants, was in three
years repealed *.

Doubts soon arose, it seems, with regard to the
construction of the remaining clause, allowing
foreign born children of *subjects* the privileges of naturalization, which induced the Parliament to pass an
Act *to explain it* †. And to effectuate this laudable
purpose the Statute of 4th George II. enacted,
" That all children who had been born out of the
ligeance of the Crown; whose *fathers* were natural
born subjects, at the time of the birth of such children, shall be deemed natural born subjects."
Thus, an act of explanation was really converted
into an act of restriction: For, the more comprehensive word, *subject*, in the Satute of Anne, was
converted

---

* By 10 Ann. chap. 5. The Palatines had flocked to
England in great numbers.
† 4 Geo. II. ch. 21.

converted, by the Statute of George, into the more restrictive term, fathers. And it added various provisos; excluding the children of attainted persons, then being in the actual service of any Prince at enmity with the Crown; and repelling particularly " the children, whose father, at the time of the birth, was liable to the penalties of treason, or felony, in case of returning into this kingdom without licence." Thus, the Statute of the 4th George II. restored the law, as it had for ages been considered from a liberal construction of the Act of Edward III. with restrictive provisos against the issue of delinquent fathers. And from this recapitulation we may reasonably conclude, that since the operation of Edward's law did not prevent whole communities from becoming aliens, when the Government of his feeble successors was overturned or withdrawn, much less can the statute of the 4th George II. save the citizens of the United States, from being regarded by our common law as aliens.

Whatever weight may be allowed to those reasonings, or to those facts, it must be admitted, that in some important points of our naval policy, the American citizens are declared to be aliens, by Act of Parliament. The statute *, " for preventing frauds in the Customs," declares, That whereas the act of navigation requires the master and three-fourths of the mariners of every *English* ship to be *English*; it is to be understood, that any of his Majesty's

* 13—14 Cha. II. ch. 11. sec. 6.

jesty's subjects of England, Ireland, or his planta
tions, are to be accounted *English, and no others.*"

Whether a theoretic problem, which seems to
lead to no practical use, merited the time, or the
ceremony, of so much investigation, is a question that may be readily asked, yet may be easily
answered. Political disquisitions, which have no
tendency to promote the ends of just Government,
by making rulers wiser, or subjects happier, ought
doubtless to be avoided, at least by wise and good
men, as speculations, idle and unprofitable. Yet,
it must be allowed to be a consideration of great
practical utility, if it could be determined with
reasonable certainty, who are the subjects of the
state, during peace, and its aliens, in war; that
we may be enabled to distinguish clearly treacher-
ous rebels from avowed enemies. The privileges,
which belong to subjects are extremely dissimilar
to the immunities that appertain to aliens: The
treatment, which humanity offers to enemies amid
the hostile contests of nations is by justice seldom
extended to rebels. And experience hath sufficiently evinced to the most inattentive observer,
that dubiousness of law is the never failing source
of public disquiet and of private misery: It is
always more easy to prevent litigation than to end
it. If those topicks of general remark should not
however be allowed decisive influence, it must be admitted, that arguments drawn from the fountain of
consequent inconvenience ought to meet with ample
discussion in the consults of wise legislators. If the

D   American

American loyalifts, who remained within the limits of the United States, even after the peace, are ftill to be regarded as fubjects, (as we have endeavoured to evince) they muft necessarily be intitled to the peculiar privileges of fubjects: They may inherit then the lands of their anceftors; they may act as merchants or as factors in the Britifh plantations; they may as mariners or mafters navigate any Britifh veffel; and they may execute any office of profit or truft, or fit in either Houfe of Parliament: And when any of thofe rights are denied them, (if we except the privilege of fitting in Parliament) they may refort to Weftminfter Hall for redrefs of fome of their wrongs; where juftice is adminiftered happily, according to the principles of rigid law, without regarding the dictates of convenient policy. But, if the American citizens are confidered as aliens they can only enjoy the more fcanty immunities, that to aliens belong: They can by no means claim the invaluable privileges, which the American loyalifts muft as fubjects be thus allowed to poffefs, in every dominion of Britain; though within the United States even thefe muft act as citizens by yielding a local fubmiffion, while they continue their refidence. The confufion in policy, in law, and in practice, which muft refult from the uncommon circumftance of two diftinct claffes of men, refiding in the fame country, yet pretending different rights, within a foreign nation, are a l fapparent, and ought all to be precluded, by meafures of precaution. To a ftate of anarchy, thus new

and

and embarraffing, it is unneceffary to add, that it has been found fufficiently difficult to man our navy, during the civil war, from the feamen infifting, that, fince they had been born in America, they could not be preffed to ferve. The bufinefs of our Cuftom-houfe requires no further perplexities, from the difficulty of knowing aliens from fubjects, under a complicated fyftem, which by the contradictory operation of new laws becomes daily more complex

Men of cautious tempers may be induced by the foregoing reafons to think, that a legiflative declaration is neceffary, to remove doubts, and to prevent difficulties. It would require only a few words in an Act of Parliament to declare, that the citizens of the United States are aliens to the Crown ; and to provide, that all perfons, who had been once Britifh fubjects and refided within any of the United States, before or at the ratification of peace, fhall be deemed Britifh fubjects, on condition, that fuch perfons fhall before or on the day of settle in any of the dominions of the Crown and take the oath of allegiance.

To a claufe, thus fimple in its creation, yet pregnant in its effect, it is not eafy to perceive what could be reafonably objected. Such a claufe would not impugn the American treaty : The legiflative declaration would rather confirm its principle and give efficacy to its meaning. Such a claufe would doubtlefs fhock the prejudices of thofe, who wifh to

imitate

imitate in refpect to the United States, that notable
policy of Cromwell *, whereby he tendered to the
cautious Hollanders the privileges of Englifhmen,
both civil and commercial. It is the eftablifhed
law however, which runs counter to thofe prejudices, working as the law does, on the new fituation, wherein nature and their own efforts had
placed the American citizens. The act of Parliament, with a wifdom which belongs to the legiflature, would nearly extinguifh the hopes of thofe
vifionary men; who flatter themfelves, that amid
the anarchical changes of the times, the United
States may defire to be admitted to a fœderal
union with Britain : and the act would greatly
allay the jealoufy of thofe American citizens, who
dread the attempts of Britain to regain by intrigue,
what fhe had been unable to effect by force. Wife
men act from juft reflection and previous concert :
The unexperienced alone apply remedies to diforders, that have already made a progrefs.

2. When the American citizens are in this manner admitted in argument, or declared by law, to be
aliens, it may be of confiderable ufe to inquire,
what immunities the law of England allows them
within

* Cromwell, fays Hume, had revived the chimerical fcheme
of a total conjunction of government, privileges, interefts,
and councils, with the United Provinces. This project appeared fo wild to the States, that they wondered any man
of fenfe could ever entertain it; and they refufed to enter
into any conferences with regard to fuch a propofal. [Hift.
8vo. ed.t. 7th v. p. 236.]

within the realm. We fhall probably find, that on this head of our jurifprudence we may juftly boaft, among the European nations, of its liberality and its wifdom. In this temper Sir Mathew Hale remarked, (and he who thinks with Hale will feldom think wrong) " that the law of England rather contracts than extends the difabilities of aliens." Every civilized fyftem has eftablifhed the convenient diftinction, which the law of England has certainly made, between aliens and fubjects ; by excluding the firft clafs from the privileges of the laft; and which we fhall fee in the refult, the American States have eftablifhed as a fundamental maxim of their free conftitutions. Yet the law of England, with a fpirit fomewhat difingenuous, allows the alien " to purchafe lands, but not to his own ufe ; fince the King is thereupon entitled to them :" And the alien can therefore maintain no action in any court of juftice, with regard to property, which the law does not allow him to hold. But, he is fully allowed to enjoy even lands for the temporary purpofe of traffick ; at the fame time that he is amply protected in his perfon, in his effects, and his reputation. That our great charter fhould have extended, by a fpecifick claufe, the fame fecurity to foreign merchants, as it prefcribes for the Liverymen of London, or the Citizens of Dublin, is a happy circumftance, which has gained our commercial fyftem the honour of Montefquieu's praife. Nor, does it detract any thing from

the

the celebration of our Englifh Juftinian *, that he granted a charter of liberties to merchant ftrangers.

From laws †, which do not merit lefs of our commendation, the American citizens may demand, as alien traders, " to be ufed within the kingdom, as merchant denizens are in other countries." And the American citizens may infift ‡ " when they come into the realm, that they be honeftly entreated as to the payment of taxes." Notwithftanding this apparent liberality merchant ftrangers were till lately fubjected in Great Britain, as they are even now in Holland and France, to thofe alien duties, which the avidity of every ftate had eftablifhed in favour of fubjects, before the fpirit of commerce had foftened the manners of mankind. The origin of thofe duties in Britain may be traced up to the unpolluted fource of the agreement of the foreign merchants themfelves, when they received their charter of liberties from the legiflative hand of Edward Ift. Merchant ftrangers are ftill fubjected, in the port of London, to feveral duties of no great burden, which belong to that opulent Corporation; the barbarous origin of which may be conjectured from the barbarifm of their appellations; of *fcavage* and *package*, of

porterage

* The Charter of Edward I. is publifhed by Molloy, in his Treatife, naval and commercial, Book ii.

† From the 9 Hen. III. ch. 9.   5 Hen IV. ch. 7.

‡ By the authority of the 12 Cha. II. ch. 4.

porterage and *water bailage*. By an act of Parliament *, which had the prevention of fraud for its end, the children of aliens are excluded, when under one and twenty years of age, from acting as merchants, or from entering goods at the Customhouse: And alien fathers are thereby precluded from sitting as jurors on the trial of causes respecting the customs; though this exclusion may be regarded by some, as a greater benefit than a disadvantage.

Under the protection of those favourable laws, without the aid of a commercial treaty, the American merchant may securely carry on his traffic: Under their friendly shade the American traveller may inspect our curiosities, or view our arts, without fear of *the droit d'aubane* of other countries; since he may dispose of his effects by testament, or the law will preserve them for his next of kin. Aliens indeed cannot in Britain, more than in any other nation, execute any office of profit or trust, or accept of any grant from the Crown, or sit in either House of Parliament †. But, from the foregoing concatenation of circumstances we may surely infer, than an alien *friend* is altogether considered as the most faithful subject, in respect to the protection of his person, his good-name, and his property; which includes nearly all his rights. And thus much with regard to those privileges and disabilities,

* 13—14 Cha. II. ch. 11. sec. 10—11.

† 12—13 Wm, III. ch. 2. sec. 3.   1 Geo. II. stat. 2 ch. 4

abilities, which the American citizens derive, as
aliens, from the operation of the law of England,
within the realm.

3. We are thence led naturally to mention
those exclusions, which result from statute, more
than from our common law, as to the external
commerce of American traders. A regard to the
national defence, by increasing the number of seamen, induced the Parliament, in the last century,
to declare *, contrary to the example of other
legislatures, that no goods shall be sent coastways
in alien-ships; that all vessels shall be deemed
foreign, except such as shall be built, within the
King's dominions, or such as shall be made prize,
under specific conditions. The Parliament were
led about the same time, by the same motives, to
prohibit all foreigners from trading with our transatlantic settlements, and our plantations from trading
with foreigners: And by the active energy of this
law, the United States were excluded, subsequent
to the epoch of their independence, from carrying
on any commerce with the British colonies and the
British colonies were thereby forbid to carry on
any commerce with them. By the act " for encouraging the Newfoundland fishery †;" which
enforced

---

* 12 ch. 2. 18. which was enforced by 7--8 Wm. III. ch. 22.

† 10—11 Wm. III. ch. 25. There is reason to suspect,
that Mr. Oswald did not much consider this law, when he
negotiated the American Peace. By the treaty the American
citizens were allowed to take any sort of fish at all the fishing
places

enforced rather than enfeebled the falutary fpirit
of that law, no alien or ftranger " can take bait or
ufe any fort of trade, or fifhing, in that ifland, or
in any of the Bays or fifhing places around it."
Owing to the prohibition of fome of thofe laws, the
American citizens cannot refide as merchants or as
factors, or execute any office of truft, within the
Britifh plantations. Yet, as foreign Proteftants
they may regain, by a feven years uninterrupted
refidence within thofe plantations, the colonial
rights, which belong to Britifh fubjects. Without that refidence, or an act of naturalization, our
traders can employ none of the American citizens
as mafters or mariners in the failing of their fhips.
And thus much with regard to the queftions,—
whether the American citizens are confidered as
aliens by our laws; what immunities are they,
as aliens, entitled to within the Kingdom; what
regulations are they governed by in their external
traffick.

§ 2. The American Affociations having in this
manner acquired independence; the American ci-

E   tizens

places of Newfoundland. But, whether the right to catch
fifh includes the right to catch bait is a doubt, which the
Dutch jurifts may anfwer. A French Statefman, when he
wanted to quarrel, would here find a fubject for quarrel.
And it would be an act worthy of the prudence of Parliament
to repeal that ftatute, as far as it tends to prevent the American States from enjoying the full right of fifhing, from a
law and a treaty ftanding oppofed to each other; in order to
evince to the world with what good faith this nation executes
the letter and the meaning of every national compact.

tizens having thus become aliens to the Crown; it was the laws rather than the government of Great-Britain, which, from the date of the peace, attentively viewed both in the exalted fituations, that both had eftablifhed for themfelves. The Britifh Government, enjoying happily no difpenfing power, could not prevent the operation of thofe Britifh laws, which had impofed difabilities and enforced reftrictions. And by accurate inquiry we fhall probably find, that the Britifh government have been hitherto only anxious to remove the various obftructions, which refentment and retaliation had thrown into the channel of our American trade.

However the nation might have felt " how fharper than a Serpent's tooth it is to have thanklefs children,"—it was furely wife in the Britifh Government to forget all the paft, when the American commerce was to be regained, if the American commerce in its greateft poffible extent be a defirable good. Animated by this worthy fpirit the Legiflature foon repealed two acts of Parliament *, which the hoftile affociations of late times had required; becaufe it was deemed " highly expedient, that the intercourfe, between Great Britain and the American States, fhould be immediately opened." The fame fenfe of expediency gave rife to a fecond act of Parliament †, which exempted American veffels from the neceffity of producing any certificate

* By 23 Geo. III. ch. 26.

† 23 Geo. III. ch. 39.

.ficate or manifeſt at the Cuſtom-houſe, except ſuch bonds as are uſually taken for the faithful exportation of goods intitled to a drawback, or a bounty ; and which empowered the King in Council, during a ſhort term, to make temporary regulatiohs for the American trade. Extraordinary as this power was, the act which conferred it may be regarded as one of the wiſeſt in the ſtatute book ; becauſe, by avoiding the dangers of " over credulous haſte," it furniſhed the intelligent with opportunities of reviewing a ſubject, complicated at once, by a conſideration of contradictory laws, and by a regard to domeſtic policy, as well as to foreign intereſts.

In purſuance of a power, thus uncommon and ſalutary, the American commerce was ere long turned into a more favourable channel than that wherein it had formerly flowed, when the United States conſtituted Britiſh Colonies. We ſhall ſee this truth, obſcure only to thoſe who ſhut their eyes, in the moſt ſtriking light, by taking two diſtinct views of our tranſatlantic trade : 1ſtly, of the exports from Great Britain to the United States : 2dly, of the imports from the United States to Britain ; as both have beeen regulated by the late proclamations.

1. By the repeal of the prohibitory acts the traders were left free to renew their former connections, or to engage in new adventures ; though no other power than the intereſt of merchants exiſted indeed, to ſtimulate the cautious, or to reſtrain the

haſty.

hafty. The proclamation of the 14th of May 1783 endeavoured, with the beft intentions though not with the beft fuccefs, to quicken mutual defire, by communicating additional motives : And by it, the fame bounties, drawbacks, and exemptions were allowed on merchandizes, which fhould be exported from Great-Britain to the United States, as are allowed to any Britifh Colony. The purpofe of this regulation was good, but the means were perhaps miftaken.

The high duties on importation are the genuine parents of drawbacks. It was foon perceived, at leaft by the traders who paid the cuftom, that a foreign commodity, when re-exported to a fecond market, muft be difpofed of dearer in proportion to the advance of every charge, or not fold at all. And hence, a regard to the profit of freights, as much as to the augmentation of failors, dictated the policy of allowing the merchant to draw back almoft the whole of the duty, which he had advanced on the import. Under the prevalence of this falutary fyftem the colonifts purchafed every European manufacture and every Eaft India luxury even cheaper than thofe commodities could be bought in Britain. But to confer this gratification on our planters required a defalcation from the public revenue of about £.100,000, a year, at the peace of 1763. And, during the preffures of that moment, it was thought prudent * " to allow no part of

the

* By 4 Geo. III. ch. 15.

the old fubfidy to be drawn back on the manufactures of Europe or Afia, which fhould in future be
fent to the Colonies, except wines, white calicoes,
and muflins." For it was known, or at leaft fuppofed, that foreign traders could enter into no competition with Britifh merchants in the markets of
the Colonies : And the ftopping of the drawbacks,
it was hoped, would impofe a tax on the planters
to the amount of the faving, which fhould be thereby
made in the Revenue. But the drawback was continued on the exports to foreign markets ; becaufe,
in their fairs Britifh traders might expect competitors. If this account fhould be allowed to be
accurate, the regulation of the 14th of May, in
refpect to drawbacks, cannot eafily be maintained to be right. And prudence, as well as juftice, requires, that there fhould be allowed the
fame drawbacks, bounties, and exemptions on
the exports to the United States, as are paid on
the commerce to other foreign countries, fince
fuch regulations would certainly be moft beneficial
to them. If we determine, from an attention to
practical effects, more than from the refult of
theoretick reafonings, we may infer, that the difadvantage of retaining five in the hundred on the
value of every cargo has been hitherto unfelt, or
perhaps it was little known.

2. From thofe difcuffions, as to the export of
our manufactures, we proceed fecondly, to re-
count the various motives, which have been in the
fame manner given to the American planters, in
order

order to induce them to fend their furplus products to Britain. By the proclamation of the
14th of May the *unmanufactured* productions of
the United States were allowed to be imported, in
Britifh, or American veffels, by any Britifh fubject,
or American citizen ; paying only the fame duties,
which Colonifts pay, even without the accuftomed
certificates : And the fame proclamation conferred
the full benefit of this order on fuch American fhips,
as had arrived, fince the 20th of January 1783.
By being thus placed on the favourable footing of
Britifh colonifts, the American citizens are exempted
not only from the payment of thofe alien duties,
which all other aliens muft pay, but even from
thofe alien duties, that were payable on the merchandize of aliens, when imported in *Britifh* fhipping. The admiffion of American oil, by the
fame proclamation, however advantageous to the
New-England fifheries and detrimental to ours,
does not merit much cenfure, or remark ; becaufe
a regard to the beft nurfery of Britifh feamen has,
by a recent order of Council, rectified the probable
overfight.

Liberality of conduct is always right : But, in
mercantile regulations it is the more laudable,
becaufe we fee, in them, the dictates of intereft fo
often preferred to the fuggeftions of policy. It is
to be regretted, that the American citizens received
unkindly the exemption from taxes, which all other
aliens muft pay. Such a reception of fuch a boon
muft excite the jealoufy of neighbouring nations,
whofe

whofe enmity or hate are of greater importance to
us. There are wife men indeed, who think, that
the abolition of the alien * duties would promote
our commercial interefts : There are intelligent perfons, who fuggeft, that the impofing of the alien
duties on *alien fhips* rather than on *alien merchandize* would augment our naval ftrength. The fen-
timents of both may be confidered as juft, in proportion as we are directed in our defires to the
accumulation of riches, or to the acquifition of
power. We boaft in vain of our religion and
liberty, of our laws and our wealth, if our fhips
are driven from our element as iflanders and we
are obliged to make conceffions to our foes, who
have lately fought us on the ocean with inferior
fleets. When the legiflators of a naval nation are
about to give encouragement, or protection, to the
induftry of their people, they ought to fix their eyes
fteadily on the feamark, which directs the national
efforts to the invigoration of ftrength, rather than
to the encreafe of opulence. And in thefe confiderations of nautical force and public fafety we
difcover the fundamental principle of the acts
of navigation; which were eftablifhed in oppofition to domeftic and foreign clamours ; which have
neverthelefs produced fo great an augmentation
of our native fhipping and failors; and which
ought therefore to be facrified to no projects of
private gain, or defires of particular gratification.

In

* The alien duties have been lately abolifhed.

In oppofition to thofe arguments, it is not eafy
to approve altogether of the meafure of allowing
the unmanufactured products of the American
States to be imported in *American veſſels*, without
paying the alien duty, while other foreign nations
continued to pay it. Who can in the leaft approve of the policy of the ftatute *, which impofed
the *alien* duty on *alien* goods when imported in
Britiſh fhips ? Both meafures were adverfe to the
principle of the acts of navigation, becaufe, however advantageous to the American citizens, both
had a tendency to diminifh the number of Britifh
fhipping and failors. On the other hand the fpirit
of thofe laws requires, that the regulation ought to
be reverfed, by impofing the alien duty on *Britiſh*
property when imported in *alien* fhips. And
urged by fimilar confiderations of felf-defence,
Sir Jofiah Child propofed upwards of a century
ago, what muft appear very extravagant in the
prefent times,—" That a law be made to impofe a
cuftom of at leaft fifty per cent. on all Eaftland
commodities, timber, boards, pipe ftaves, anp
falt, imported into England upon any fhips but
Engliſh built, or at leaft fuch as are failed with
an *Engliſh* mafter and three-fourths *Engliſh* mariners."

Thofe arguments and that authority were either
forgotten, or neglected, when the Privy Council
iffued the proclamation of the 6th of June 1783;
or perhaps that body was carried away by its
anxieties to conciliate American regard, and to regain

* 2 Geo. II. chap. 34. fec. 20.

gain a long loft trade, which for years had been loudly reprefented as the only commerce worthy of our care. It is not fo eafy to difcover the neceffity or the ufe of that part of the proclamation, which exprefsly permits the importation of naval ftores. By the regulation of the 14th of May they feem to have been allowed a free importation, under the general terms *unmanufactured products*:— For, pitch, tar, and turpentine, mafts, yards, and bowfprits, and even indigo, which is equally enumerated, cannot be brought to the place of exportation in any lower ftate of manufacture, than that wherein they have always been fold. Enumerations, which follow general words, always create doubts where none exifted before; while comprehenfive defcriptions, that follow particular enumerations, only enlarge the rule, without creating a difficulty. The cuftom-houfe officers have already had occafion to afk, if pot-afh be an unmanufactured product? It is to be regretted, that our great lexicographer did not find the word *unmanufactured* in any of the Englifh claffics, fince its various ufe might have eftablifhed its different meaning. The ftatute of the 8th George I. has applied to timber the epithets *wrought* or *unwrought*, whilft the fame law, with a prudence which belongs to the legiflature, enumerated the various goods, that, in mercantile language, are denominated *lumber*. In vain we feek for words fufficiently accurate to convey the idea of allowing the importation of American products, as they come from the foil, almoft in

F   their

their natural ſtate, yet excluding ſuch American merchandize, as have undergone the diſcipline of manufacture. And it would therefore be prudent, when the Parliament is about to eſtabliſh a ſyſtem for the American trade, to enumerate all thoſe American productions, which good policy may allow to be imported in future; and which may be found in the Inſpector General's books and would form no long catalogue. That meaſure may be regarded as ſalutary, which has a tendency to prevent diſputes on the one ſide and difficulties on the other.

It may be moreover remarked, as to the proclamation of the 6th of June, that this nation has paid on the various articles enumerated in it, when imported from the colonies, upwards of a million and a half, ſince the bounty was firſt given, during the reign of Anne: On naval ſtores

from 1706 to 1729   —   £. 430,178 ;

from 1729 to 1774   —   1,028,584 ;

and on indigo   ———   145,022 ;

£. 1,583,784.

It is one of the many benefits, which the wiſdom of our councils may derive from the independence of the United States, that the bounties, which had thus drawn ſo vaſt a ſum from the public revenue, have now happily ceaſed*. An attention to onr manufactures

---

* Thoſe bounties expired on the 24th of June 1781.— But, had the United States continued Britiſh Colonies a deſire

manufactures of cloth has exempted indeed all indigo from the payment of taxes on the importation : But, there are various taxes, which may be diftinctly feen in the book of rates, collected on pitch, tar, and turpentine, mafts, yards, and bowfprits, when introduced from any European nation, together with the alien duties, when thefe cumbrous commodities are fetched in foreign fhips †. It is apparent then, that all thofe taxes became payable, by operation of law, on the import of American naval ftores, from the moment wherein the United States were admitted to be independent : It is equally plain, that it was the proclamations before mentioned, which fufpended the operation of thofe laws and the collection of thofe duties. And Great Britain thereby conferred a benefit on the United States, by withholding fomething from her revenue, and by rifquing the refentment of her powerful neighbours. Great-Britain at the fame time conferred another favour on the United States of no fmall importance to them. While the bounties were withdrawn, by the admiffion of independence, the proclamation exempted American wood from thofe duties, which

F 2 are

fire to gratify them would have continued the bounties; as indeed the exemption from duties may be regarded as a bounty of an inferior kind, which operates againft the importers of European commodities of the fame nature.

† See the volume compiled by Meffrs. Sims and Frewin, under the directions of the Commiffioners of the Cuftoms, and publifhed in 1782.

are payable on the import of wood from the rivers of Germany and the fhores of the Baltic. It was probably known, that the importers of European lumber, for the ufe of the builder, had underfold the American, even when the bounties were paid. And it was perhaps deemed prudent to preferve, by exempting the American lumber from duties, a flight competition in the domeftic market, between Europe and America, in the fale of their wooden products.

But, as indigo has been exempted from taxes, by a regard to our dyers, the argument appears much ftronger for freeing from cuftoms every fpecies of naval ftores, whether of the product of Europe, or America, from a refpect, which is much more due to our fhipwrights and coopers: The dyers and workers in wool may augment our opulence; but, the carpenters and coopers contribute to our fafety. And thus we perceive, that the Britifh Government has looked with no inimical eye towards America, fince the peace eftablifhed irrevocably the independence of the United States, as every wife man ought to wifh.

If that truth required any confirmation we fhould find proofs enow in the orders of Council, whereby the introduction of American tobacco was regulated. By the proclamation of the 6th of June the moft ancient branch of our colony commerce was re-eftablifhed on the fame ground, whereon it had flourifhed for ages before the revolt: And by it the importation of tobacco was
allowed,

allowed, either in Britifh or American fhips, on paying 5 *per cent.* of the value, and on giving bond for the payment of all other duties at a future day. But, the war had produced a variety of new regulations, with a fucceffion of additional taxes. And when the approach of peace opened a profpect of the renewment of traffick, it foon became apparent, that to carry on the commerce of tobacco would require a greater capital than any traders choofe to depofit at the Cuftom-houfe, in hopes of confequential gains. It was owing to thefe reafons probably, that the Privy Council iffued a fecond proclamation on the 5th of November laft; allowing American tobacco to be imported into London, Briftol, and Liverpool, into Cowes, Whitehaven, and Greenock, on giving bond, as well for the Old Subfidy of 5 *per cent.* before mentioned, as for all other duties; and fecuring the commodity under the King's locks, till the importer fhould want it for domeftic confumption or foreign fupply.

Thefe proclamations feem thus to have eftablifhed the fame regulation, which the tobacco Colonies had ardently prayed for in 1732; and which Walpole certainly intended to grant, by his famous excife fcheme, till he was ftunned by clamour and overpowered by violence. The planters had often feen and fometimes felt, that in proportion as the Britifh merchants advanced their money for taxes, the charges on the merchandize were raifed, till by enhancing the expences, the ultimate fale of the tobacco did not repay the original

labour

labour. And the Aſſemblies ſolicited the Parliament for the privilege of placing the commodity
under the King's locks, on giving bond for the
payment of the duties at a ſubſequent day: But,
their ſolicitations were diſappointed by the intereſted oppoſition of the tobacco factors, more than
by the unwillingneſs of the Legiſlature*. In this
manner has there been lately eſtabliſhed a beneficial regulation of tobacco, which had been denied
by our factions to coloniſts, yet has been now
granted by our good ſenſe to foreigners, who had
no

---

* The Aſſembly of Virginia ſent Sir John Randolph to
England, in 1732, to ſolicit a ſimilar regulation, which was
however then exploded as an exciſe, ſince the officer was empowered to inſpect the tobacco in the warehouſe. In the
ſubſequent year the ſame Aſſembly tranſmitted an Addreſs to
the King; thanking his Majeſty for the countenance he had
given the Colony on that occaſion;—" And though unfortunate for them (ſaid they) that their intereſts and the intereſts
of thoſe, whoſe oppoſition prevailed, were irreconcileable,
they had abundant reaſon to admire his Majeſty's juſtice and
conſtancy, when no clamour how univerſal ſoever, could
change his good purpoſes, or divert his deteſtation of fraud,
however diſguiſed and ſupported by names and ſounds."—
The Miniſters of that day thought it prudent to ſuppreſs the
latter part of the Addreſs, which reflected on Sir John Bar-
nard and his coadjutors, who had diſappointed, by their
oppoſition, the prayer of the Aſſembly. Yet, the Virginia
Aſſembly were lately the firſt to declare commercial hoſtility
againſt Great Britain, on account of the Weſt-India regulations; though the Virginians could not know indeed, in
December, of the order of the 5th of November preceding,
which did not arrive in America, till the 6th of February
1784.

no claim on our kindnefs. While every facility was thus given to the importation of American tobacco we have ftrengthened the laws, for preventing the growth of tobacco in Britain, which it had been found fo difficult to enforce during the laft century; as our farmers thought it their intereft to rear tobacco at home. And by this means the American planters poffefs a double monopoly of this great article of traffic; the Britifh landholder cannot raife it on Britifh ground; the Britifh confumer cannot import it from Portugal or Spain, fince the duties payable on Spanifh or Portugueze tobacco amount nearly to a prohibition.

In fuperaddition to all thofe meafures, which have thus removed every obftruction from the flow of our American trade, may be mentioned the proclamation of the 5th of September laft, which adminiftered no fmall facility to practical bufinefs. This order directed, that all thofe bonds, which our commercial laws had required for the prevention of fraud, might be cancelled by producing certificates of the performance from any Naval Officer, or Magiftrate, of the United States. And by thofe various proclamations has the trade between Great Britain and the United States been opened and encouraged on the part of this nation. In the wide circle of commerce, complicated as it is by the taxes and reftrictions which avarice and jealoufy have impofed, there is not to be found a traffick, fo liberal in its policy and fo unreftrained

in

in its vent, as the trade, which now runs free and full in its courfe between this kingdom and the United States. The practical refult has amply juftified the previous policy, which had for its means, protection and freedom. An unexampled export of our manufactures has been made during the laft feafon to the United States; a correfpondent confignment hath followed from them to Britain, of almoft all the furplus products of the Southern States, which had not been fold by the growers: And hence the American factors, who had fettled in Holland and France, during the war, have lately been obliged to follow the commerce, which had given them employment and wealth. Recent experience hath fhewn them, what they might have inferred from their former knowledge, that London muft neceffarily be the American mart. It is an additional proof of the validity of the foregoing reafonings, that none of thofe, who have been ftudious to detect faults and forward to expofe them, have objected any thing to the beforementioned regulations, except one writer indeed, who infifts, *That the authors of them have difplayed unufual timidity and caution.*

But, no one has found *timidity* and *caution*, which the wife will not think very blameable qualities, either in the credits lately given to the American citizens, or in the regulations of the commerce between the Britifh Weft-Indies and the United States. This is the meafure that alone appears to

have

have raised any clamour.   The West-India trade
was regulated by the Proclamation, dated the 2d
of July 1783; which is said to be "founded on
gross misinformation;" which is censured by the
American letter writer, "As a system derogatory
to the honour, degrading to the spirit, and inju-
rious to the interests of a great people." Facts
however ought always to be fairly stated before
faults should ever be imputed.   Let us in this
spirit examine the Proclamation, which has thus
given rise to controversy, and which has at once
incited the complaints of the West-India planter
and the resentment of the American citizen.   It
directs, 1stly, That pitch, tar, turpentine, hemp and
flax, yards, bowsprits, staves, heading, boards,
timber, shingles, and every other species of timber,
and also horses, neat cattle, sheep, hogs, poultry,
and all other kinds of live stock, and live provisions, pease, beans, potatoes, wheat, flour, bread,
biscuit, rice, oats, barley and all other grain, being the product of the United States, may be imported into any of the West-India Islands, by
British subjects, in *British ships:* It allows 2dly,
That rum, sugar, molasses, coffee, cocoa-nuts,
ginger, and pimento, may, in the *same manner* and
by the *same persons*, be sent from the British West-
Indies to the United States, upon payment of the
same duties and liable to the same regulations, as if
the same articles were cleared at the Custom-house
for any British Colony.   Of a subject so interesting, because it involves in its discussion the safety

of

of the empire, let us take two diftinct views: 1ftly, As the Proclamation affects the American States; 2dly, As it concerns the Britifh Weft-Indies.

1. The connection between the various Colonies of the American Empire of Britain arofe affuredly from their being territories of the fame ftate. The moment the Independence of the United States was recognized, they became foreign countries with regard to the remaining Plantations of Britain: And the citizens of the one and the planters of the other, who had once been fellow-fubjects of the fame community, became aliens with refpect to each other. The acts of Parliament, which prohibited all future commerce between regions that had once been bound in the fame compact, only enforced the original fyftem, which the law of nations had always enjoined*. It requires only a fhort recapitulation to trace up the rife of that fyftem to its true fource. The policy of Spain, fays the great Bacon, was to keep the trade of the Indies under fuch lock and key, as both confederates, yea, and fubjects, were excluded of commerce unto thofe countries; fuch a vigilant dragon is there that keepeth the golden-fleece. Portugal, who

---

* The Weft-India Committee have furmifed, rather than infilled, that by the Freeport Act of the prefent reign the people of Jamaica may import all the merchandizes of the United States, which are *foreign Colonies*: But, the United States have been admitted by the world to be *fovereign* and confequently cannot be *fubordinate*, which is an effential quality of all Colonies.

who purfued difcovery with equal fleps, catched
the jealous fpirit of Spain. France and England,
who followed both at the diftance of a century,
adopted the flattering, becaufe exclufive example of
both. And thus, *it became a fundamental law of
Europe,* fays Montefquieu, *that all, traffic with a
foreign Colony fhall be regarded as a mere monopoly:*
Hence, continues that celebrated jurift, it is likewife acknowledged, *that a commerce between the
Mother Countries does not include a permiffion to trade
with their Colonies.* When Great Britain recognized
the fovereignty of the United States and declared in
the face of the world, *that we are at peace with
each other,* this declaration gave the United States
no right to trade to her Plantations, or even to
fifh on her coafts.

On the law of nations, thus eftablifhed and
known, the French fecurely relied, when they entered into treaty with the United States, in
February 1778. But, the Dutch, fufpicious from
fenfe of weaknefs, or guided by charaTeriftic caution, inferted an exprefs ftipulation, in their Treaty
of OTober 1782, "That the United States fhall
leave the States General the peaceable enjoyment
of their rights, in the countries, iflands, and feas,
in the Eaft and Weft-Indies, without moleftta-
tion." Great Britain preferred the confident policy of France to the fcrupulous attention of Holland; as it did not probably occur to the wifefl of
our ftatefmen, that when the United States fhould
be admitted into the community of nations, they
would,

would by their conduct, much more than by their words, refuse obedience to the law of all civilized nations. Yet, confidence in one's own title has seldom been construed into an admission of its invalidity. And we may therefore conclude, that Great Britain enjoyed from the date of the peace as much right as Denmark or France, Portugal or Spain, to regulate her own Plantations; since there is no positive provision in the treaty to repel the general inferences of law.

Nevertheless the proclamation of the 2d of July 1783 ; which permitted British subjects to transport in British ships the West-India Commodities to the United States and to carry their most useful products in return ; which thus conferred many benefits on the United States, though not every benefit ; has been declared by some of those States " to be inconsistent with the rights of free trade." The American governments then, not the American mobs, claim *the right of free trade* with the transatlantic settlements of Spain, Portugal and France, as much as with the plantations of Britain. But, let us inquire, whence do they derive this new pretension ? From the law of Nature ? No. Every independent Community has a right indeed, in virtue of it's natural liberty, to trade with those *who shall be willing to correspond with such intentions ;* and to molest it in the the exercise of this right is an injury. But, though every one has a right *to traffick with those who are willing* ; yet, says Vattel, every Sovereign State may decline a commerce

which

which is dangerous, or even difadvantageous; and
has confequently full power to determine for itfelf
what is ufeful, or unfalutary: It may receive therefore, or refufe, any commercial overtures from foreigners, without giving them a pretence to accufe
it of injuftice, or to demand a reafon for fuch re-
fufal, much lefs to make ufe of compulfion or
threats. Do the American governments claim the
right of free trade from the law of nations? They
can not. Colonies are the offspring of Society,
during that period of refinement, which the prevalence of the commercial fpirit fuppofes. And
by the confent of the civilized communities of the
European world, it was early eftablifhed, (as we
have already feen) that the fovereignty as well as
the traffick of every plantation fhould exclufively
belong to the State which had formed it. The law
of nations therefore, which is only the original confent and continual practice of nations, has prohibited the intercourfe of one foreign country with
the colonies of all other foreign countries. And a
free trade with an American Colony of confequence
never exifted. Thus, while the American governments claim the rights of a free trade with the Britifh plantations they virtually avow their purpofe
to difregard the law of Nature as well as of nations,
which by treaty, or by implication, has regulated
univerfal trade and with it the conventions of all
public bodies.

Whatever extravagance the American populace
may commit, contrary to their genuine interefts,

the

the American politicians would do well to inquire, before they violate public decorum, how they have been wronged, by the commercial policy, which Britain has continued rather than adopted, in respect to her own plantations. The most ignorant of the American Lawyers will instruct their countrymen, that they may feel an inconvenience without suffering an injury; while the world shall consider every wrong as an unjust deprivation of some previous right. But, what American right was infringed when Great Britain denied to the American citizens a direct trade, in their own ships, to the British colonies? While Great Britain allowed her laws to operate on the American States, as foreign countries, she only did that which other European powers continued to do. Portugal and Spain have excluded from their colonies the American traders with a jealousy peculiar to both. France indeed has granted to her American allies a petty participation in her West India commerce, which, as far as suited her convenience, they always enjoyed. From Britain the United States were certainly entitled to justice, but not surely to favour : Yet, it was no inconsiderable benefit, which Britain conferred on them, and which no European nation enjoys, when she suspended the rigorous operation of those laws, that prevented even British merchants from sending the products of the United States directly to the British West Indies, or the produce of the West Indies immediately to the United States. When the Spaniards lately imprisoned prifoned the American traders at the Havannah, becaufe they dreaded their intrigues; when the French, in order to effectuate their policy, at the fame time confined the American navigators, failing around Hifpaniola in queft of markets, to Cape Francois ; the American citizens probably fighed in fecret, but they did not avow refentment, or threaten retaliation. Thus, an inconvenience may be felt, though no wrong may be done. When good fenfe fhall have triumphed over vulgar prejudice we may reafonably hope, the American Philofophers will teach their followers, that having manfully gained the bleffings of a free and equal ftation, among the powers of the earth, they ought to fuffer patiently the embarraffments, which every where refult from greatnefs. A little oppofition, far lefs adverfity, will inftruct the American governments, that they ought to pay fome deference to the municipal rules of other Sovereign Powers ; becaufe they flatter their own vanity of independence, when they conform to the regulations, which other independent States may think fit to eftablifh.

But, whatever meafure the American Congrefs and Affemblies may choofe to adopt, the intereft of the American planters will furnifh Great Britain with the beft fecurity for their good behaviour. To fend traders to purchafe the lumber, that they clear from their lands, and to carry away the corn and cattle, which they raife on their fields, can furely be thought no great injury, far lefs in-

fult,

fult, to any community: Nor, can it be deemed
any great difadvantage to the American planters to
fend them abundant fupplies of rum, fugar, molaffes, and other neceffary products of the Weft-
India iflands. The American people, "who have
feldom wandered widely from their intereft," are
fully aware, that it is demand and fupply, which
regulate the prices in every market. They already
perceive, that their chief advantage confifts, in
having in their ports many fellers of the goods
which they may want to buy, and many buyers of
what they may wifh to fell; that to exclude the
traders of any one country, or defcription, would
amount to a permiffion to the favoured traders to
raife their prices againft every buyer and to fink
them againft every feller: And the planters have
not to learn, that favourites feldom confer favours,
fince they have generally few friends. The planters can therefore derive no benefit from the exclufion
of any one clafs of traders, were the propofal even
to come from the merchants of Bofton, New-York,
or Philadelphia, of Baltimore, or Charles-Town,
which would form a monopoly in favour of the
few againft the many, by facrificing the agricultural
intereft to the mercantile. Though the American
merchants might gain, by exclufive projects, the
American planters are only interefted, in having a
a competition, in their markets, between buyers
and fellers of various countries and therefore of
various views.

From

From the foregoing reasonings we may surely infer, that the Assemblies of Virginia and Maryland acted contrary to the genuine interests of their constituents, when the one resolved, That no *British* ship should import the produce of the West-Indies, and the other imposed a tax of three shillings sterling the ton of every *British* vessel: When the other Assemblies concurred generally with both, in the resolution of arming the Congress with power over commerce, for the purpose of retaliation, or redress, they equally sacrificed the real advantage of their country to their own resentments. But, revenge is merely a momentary passion, while avarice is the most obstinate affection of the mind. Cool calculation will ere long discover, that were the West India traffic wholly cut off, the planters would certainly lose a market for their provisions and lumber of the annual value of half a million; the commonwealth would moreover be deprived of a yearly balance of £.350,000; which is payable in bullion on that branch of business, while specie does not abound among them. By that determination the Assemblies would at once raise Canada and Nova-Scotia from the ground and execute that measure, which wise men wish for, as the system that great Britain ought spontaneously to adopt.

2. From investigations with respect to the manner wherein the American citizens are interested, either individually, or collectively, by the late regulations of the American trade, we are led secondly to discuss

H   the

the various ways, in which the Weft-Indies may be affected by the proclamation of the 2d of July 1783. Let us firft ftate the fact and then draw the inferences. Like the American citizens the Weft India planters complain, with equal propriety, not fo much, that the proclamation did not give them many advantages, as that it did not give them every advantage. The laws forbade them to carry on any commerce with the United States; yet, the Weft-Indians clamour, becaufe they were only allowed to traffick in *Britifh* fhips: They are permitted to fend their rum, fugar, molaffes, and other products to the American markets and to bring the moft material of the American produce in return; yet, are they diffatisfied, becaufe they are not moreover allowed to employ *American* fhips; without confidering how much the permiffion would enervate the nautical ftrength of Britain, whereon they rely for defence. It is not uncommon to fee men carried away by their prefent paffion to their ultimate ruin. When the Weft-Indians beheld, with too favourable eyes the revolt of the Colonifts, they might have forefeen, that forcible oppofition would probably end in abfolute independence:—When the Weft-Indians, by their clamours, confirmed the purpofe of the revolted colonies, little did they perceive, that fuccefs would convert fellow-fubjects into enemies, during war, and into aliens, in peace.

Yet, the Committee of Weft-India Planters and merchants now reprefent: " That the permiffion

of

of American ſhips, as heretofore, freely to bring the produce of the American States to the Sugar Iſlands and to take back the produce of our iſlands in return is *obviouſly eſſential.*" With deference to ſuch reſpectable authority it may yet be aſſerted, that the Weſt-India planters and merchants did not always argue thus. Many years have not paſſed away ſince their predeceſſors caſt the Continental Coloniſts the gauntlet of defiance. When the Weſt-India planters applied to Parliament, in 1731, for protection againſt the ſmugglers of the Northern colonies they as confidently ſtated*, " That there are perſons ſtill living, who very well remember, ſince there were very great quantities of proviſions and other requiſites for planting ſent from *Old* England to our ſugar colonies, becauſe at that time our continent colonies were not fully able to ſupply them." Nevertheleſs are we now told by the ſame authority, that the plantations of the South and North *were ſettled with deſign to ſatisfy each others wants.* Thus, we behold the Weſt-Indians of 1731 ſtand oppoſed to the Weſt-Indians of 1783, with the contradictorineſs of men, who ſacrifice oftener at the ſhrine of intereſt than in the temple of conſiſtency.

From hiſtory we may learn indeed, that **Old** England hath ſucceſſively furniſhed all her tranſatlantic ſettlements with every neceſſary for planting. When the Parliament prohibited †, in 1663, the

direct

---

* Anderſ. Chron. Com. 2 v. p. 336.
† By 15 Cha. II. chap. 7.

direct importation into the Britifh colonies of *foreign* commodities, being the growth of Europe, the law exprefsly provided, that horfes and *victual* of the product of Scotland and Ireland might be tranfported thence to the plantations. The term *victual* carries with it fo large a meaning in our language, as well as in our laws, that it includes " all ftores for the fupport of life." And from that early epoch of our colonization horfes and victual have been conftantly fent from Ireland and Scotland to the Britifh Weft-Indies.— From a querulous pamphlet, which, when publifhed, in 1689, was entitled *The Groans of the Plantations*, we may learn not only the caufe* of their *groans*, but alfo the courfe of their fupplies, at the æra of the Revolution. "We have our horfes from England, faid the Weft-Indians; the bread we eat is of Englifh flour; we take great quantities of Englifh beer and of Englifh cheefe and butter: we fit by the light of Englifh candles: Moreover, we take thoufands of barrels of Irifh beef." More moderate in their defires, becaufe they were lefs opulent than the Weft-Indians of 1784, the Weft-Indians of 1689 " were well contented to be confined to England only, for thofe things that England doth produce."

The

---

* They had then two caufes of complaint; the late tax upon fugar, which was the firft, and the acts of navigation, which confined their exports to England: And the Weft-Indians have profpered and groaned ever fince.

The Continental Colonifts foon fupplied themfelves and gradually circumvented the Englifh merchants, in the Weft-India markets. Sir Jofiah Child faw the rivalry begin, during the reign of Charles II. and warned the nation of the confequences. Dr. D'Avenant beheld its progrefs, amid the wars of William III. and vainly urged the interpofition of the Legiflature. While the Britifh landholders were at a vaft expence defending the colonies, during every conteft fince the Revolution, the colonial landholders entered into a too fuccefsful competition withtheir protectors, in every port, during peace; nay, even fupplied with provifions the enemies of both, in war. The colonifts were regarded as fellow-fubjects, who merited not only defence, but indulgence. The landholders of Britain allowed a double monopoly againft themfelves: They permitted the Weft-Indians to furnifh them with all things from the continental colonies; they indulged the Weft-Indians with the fole fupply of the Britifh markets, for rum, fugar, and their other products. But, though our kindnefs, rather than our interefts, allowed to the continental colonifts a competition in every market, our policy ought not to permit aliens to act as rivals in the commerce of the Britifh Weft-Indies, which the Britifh nation is ftill bound to defend. The French do not act in this manner: And yet, the Weft-India regulations of France are by all the world commended.

We

We shall nevertheless be pertinaciously told
" That the admission of American ships into the
West-India ports is *obviously essential*: That Great-
Britain must at last submit." These are at least
confident words. The term *obviously* supposes,
that the general assertion admits of no controversy :
And the word *essential* signifies that the nature of
the grievance allows no alleviation. The continental colonists, when on the eve of a revolt, in
the same manner thought, that their traffic was
obviously essential to the West-Indians ; and therefore prohibited all commerce between them. Yet,
eight years experience hath evinced, contrary to
malignant speculation, that it is possible for the
West-Indies to exist and to prosper, were the
United States doomed to perpetual sterility. It
is the mercantile spirit which brings the buyers and
sellers of distant countries together. Merchants
are sufficiently studious to discover the demands of
every market ; that they may profit, by supplying
them. The traders of Great-Britain and Ireland
seized the opportunity, which the factious folly of
the Americans had furnished, to revive and extend the business, that had enriched their fathers,
during happier times. Even during a consuming
war, when vast fleets and armies were fed beyond
the ocean, Great-Britain and Ireland sufficiently
supplied all those necessaries, which the West-
Indians did not readily find in their own œconomy.
Their superabundance even furnished the army
that General Grant conducted to their aid with
several

feveral months provifions. And the fleet too fometimes partook in what the planters had to fpare. The following cuftom-houfe entries will fhew fufficiently, whence that abundance was drawn, at the beginning, the middle, and at the end of the war.

Of SALTED PROVISIONS there were exported from England alone:

	Irish Beef. Barrels.	Irish Pork. Barrels.	English Beef and Pork. Barrels.	Total Barrels	English Bacon. Flitches.	English Tripe. Kegs.
In 1773	1195	383	259	1,787	558	306;
In 1780	9844	3471	4480	17,795	3369	1582;
In 1783	9848	3059	3619	16,526	5188	2559;

Contrast with those quantities the West India supply of Beef and Pork from the revolted colonies according to an average of three years ending with 1773, — 14992

Of PICKLED FISH there were exported from England only:

	Red Herrings. Barrels.	White Ditto. Barrels.	Total. Barrels.	Pilchards. Hogsheads.	Salmon. Barrels.
In 1773	514	1876	2390	211	5.
In 1780	1816	7281	9097	1188	109.
In 1783	2840	15060	17900	313	35.

Contrast with these, the West-India supply of pickled fish from the revolted colonies, according to an average of three years, ending with 1773, 16200

From England only there were exported of BUTTER, CHEESE, and BEER:

	Irish Butter. Hund. weight.	English Ditto. Firkins.	English Cheese Hund. weight.	Beer. Tons.
In 1773	1195	92	3247	1881
In 1780	9844	274	3660	2042
In 1783	3195	522	4475	3170

With the laft-mentioned products of our fields
we find little from the revolted Colonies to con-
traft, becaufe in thefe they had little competition.
From thofe entries, with all their defects, it is fufficiently clear, that Great Britain had regained the
fupply of thofe articles, and that, as to thofe neceffaries the Weft India demand was amply anfwered.
The planters derived ground provifions from that
beft of all refources, their own diligence and attention. And their meafure of all things was probably
filled up from the prizes, which hoftility conducted
to their ports. But it was from the embarraffments,
which their affected friends intended to throw in
their way, that the Weft Indians learned a leffon
of the greateft importance for every people to
know, that no community ought to depend on its
neighbours, for what the neceffities of life require.
The country, which is *phyfically* dependent on
another, muft foon become *politically* dependent
on it.

If indeed the admiffion of American veffels into
the Weft India ports were effential to the furnifhing of the unhappy Negroes with food, benevo-
lence would drop a tear over the wants of human
nature, and juftice would grant what policy might
wifh to deny. The queftion however does not
turn on the pivot of fupplying the Weft India
Lords with their ufual luxuries, or the Weft India flaves with their accuftomed needs. The proclamation has provided, that both fhall be fupplied in the moft *reafonable* manner, having at once

I
an

an attention to private convenience and to public safety : But, the West Indians contend, that they ought to be accommodated, in the moſt *profitable* manner, having a regard to their own intereſt alone. And we have ſeen, that three abundant markets, namely, Great-Britain, and Ireland, in Europe, and Newfoundland, Canada, and Nova Scotia, in America, had been already opened, when the proclamation added the United States as a fourth. True indeed, neither the proclamation nor the law commanded traders *to ſupply the Weſt India wants.* It was thought ſufficient, that the laws and the proclamation removed every hindrance, All ſyſtems preſume, that it is the buſineſs of merchants to diſcover the neceſſities of mankind and to ranſack the earth for the means of gratification. The traders have actually found means, ſince the peace, as they had already done, during the war, to accommodate the Weſt Indies abundantly. Almoſt every letter by every packet communicates the welcome news of plentiful markets. And it is a deciſive confirmation of the truth of private intelligence and of public report, that thoſe who have clamoured the moſt have brought no incontrovertible evidence of an exiſting neceſſity. Thus, the meaſure of admitting the American veſſels into the Weſt-India ports reſults at laſt into a mere point of politics, or conſideration of mercantile profit. The pretenſion of the Weſt Indians, which can conſequently be no more conſidered as a claim of neceſſity, or of juſtice, has been run out by the ingenuity

genuity of men into various modifications of demand and supply. It has been suggested by some, that were the United States to prohibit all traffick with the British West Indies, the best market for the products of both would be in future cut off. By others it has been confidently said, that were that event to take place, the Continental Colonies, which still belong to Britain, would soon be able to supply the void. And a third class of men, with a bolder spirit insist, that the only inquiry should be, whether the British West-Indies can find suitable markets on the face of the earth, without regarding the United States, or even our remaining plantations, any more than if they did not exist. In order to discover all the distinct shades of truth, which may be contained in each of those propositions, it is intended to consider the difficult subject, under three distinct heads, in their order: 1stly, Whence can the British West Indies be supplied with provisions and other necessaries, if the United States should deny their aid; 2dly, Whence can the West Indies be furnished with lumber, or timber, wrought and unwrought, for the various uses of the cooper and builder; and 3dly, Whence will the West Indians find consumption for their rum and other luxurious productions, if the United States should reject them.

1. An inquiry into the state of population in the British West India Islands may be regarded as rather curious than useful, when the amount of their consumption can be nearly ascertained by

I 2   facts.

facts. The Board of Trade reported to the House of Lords, in 1734, that the number of white men was then 36,201. If we suppose that they have doubled in half a century, by whatever means, the present white inhabitants may be calculated at about 72,000 souls. Mr. Glover, who very ably pled the cause of the West Indians before the House of Commons, in 1775, roundly stated the number of Negroes at rather more than 400,000. If we admit the foregoing conjectures to be nearly the truth, it cannot be surely inferred, that seventy-two thousand masters, with four hundred thousand slaves, form a community of sufficient bulk, to whose gratifications the interest and even independence of the nation ought to be sacrificed. They exist in a state of society extremely analogous to the situation of Europe, during feudal times: And like the Barons and their vassals, during the infancy of agriculture, the West Indians consume great quantities of salted provisions. From the revolted Colonies they received of

BEEF and PORK.

In 1771———13,511 barrels.
72——12,575
73——18,890

An annual demand of 14,992 barrels was doubtless a considerable quantity: Yet, from Ireland alone the West Indies may be furnished with greater supplies of salted beef and pork than they

can

[61]

can ever confume; as we may learn from the following ſtatement *

* The public are indebted for many of the Cuſtom-houſe accounts, which will frequently occur in the following ſheets, and which are intereſting, becauſe they are accurate, to Mr. Irving; a gentleman, who poſſeſſes more commercial detail than Doctor D'Avenant, with as much genius for the regulation of Cuſtom-houſe practice.

 From

• From the United States there were exported, in the year 1772.

Beef and pork - 20,332 barrels, the beef at 28s. per barrel, and pork at 40s.

Hams - 1107 barrels, 6d. per lb.
Butter - 1179 cwt. $£.2: 10s.$ per lb.

* From Ireland there were exported, according to an average of seven years, ending with 1777.

Beef - 195,605 barrels, at $£.1: 12s.$ per barrel.
Pork   55,240   at 2: 0
           250,845

Bacon 19,125 flitches at 15s. per cwt.
Butter $£67,212$ cwt. at 2: 5s. 6d per cwt.

Pork, Irish—none
Hams ——— 0 0 6 per lb.
Flitches ——— 0 0 5½ per lb.
Butter, American ——— 0 0 9 per lb.
Butter, Irish ——— 0 0 10¼ per lb.

Yet, the unexampled severity of the preceding Winter may have operated on all those prices.

* The detail of Irish provisions was taken from Mr. A. Young's Tour in Ireland: The American account is from the inspector of import and exports books. Let us contrast the above-mentioned prices, with the prices current of the same articles at Baltimore, the great mart of the middle States, in May 1784; converting the currency to sterling at 66⅔; namely.

Beef, American $£.2$ 5 0 per barrel.
Beef, Irish   1 16 0 per ditto
Pork, American   3 12 0 per ditto

Thus, by contrasting the whole quantities of those different kinds of salted provisions, which were exported from Ireland and the United States, about the same time, we see such a superiority in the first market over the second, as to leave the merchant little room for choice. The Irish supply is vastly greater; the prices are nearly equal; yet it must be observed, that the Irish barrel is somewhat smaller, while the quality is infinitely preferable. Considering how much our West-India vessels have hitherto wanted freights, and how commodious the ports of Ireland are to the shipping from the Western coast of Britain, the salted provisions of Ireland may be thence transported cheaper to the West Indies, than from the nearer shores of the United States. And the Irish beef and pork and butter were always preferred in the West India markets, and even in the markets of the revolted Colonies. Britain too, we have seen, can furnish no inconsiderable quantity of all those articles. To preserve the supplying of salted provisions to Britain and Ireland, by excluding the competition of the United States was the ruling principle of the late regulations. And thus from the independence of the revolted Colonies have we gained all the benefits of the supply and the still more important advantage of the freights.

The wisdom of that regulation, and the advantages which Britain will gain from that signal event, will appear in a still clearer light, if we take a comprehensive view of our fisheries; which, as the

best

beſt nurſery of our ſeamen, are ſo worthy of our care.

The following detail is a ſketch of the Newfoundland fiſhery, during the year 1771.

Britiſh fiſhing veſſels (of which 244 on the Great Bank fiſhing)		269 ſhips
Britiſh trading veſſels	—	120
American ditto	—	125
	Total	614 ſhips

Tonnage of Britiſh trading and fiſhing veſſels	—	32,949 tons
Ditto of the American	—	8,475
	Total	41,424 tons

Number of men in the Britiſh *Fiſh-ing* veſſels	—	4,477
Ditto in the Britiſh *trading* veſſels		1,118
Ditto in the American trading veſſels		865
Fiſhermen, Shoremen, and paſſen-gers from Britain and Ireland		5,529
Inhabitants who remained, during the winter	— —	6,913
Men employed in this fiſhery		18,902

The

The number of boats, employed
   by fishing ships   —   556
Yearly from Britain and Ireland,
   and having no share in vessels
   fishing on the Great Bank   —   559
The number of boats employed by
   inhabitants   ——   1,173

              Number of boats   2,288

The quintals of fish made in fishing
   ships   —   —   236,000
Ditto in bye boats   —   147,999
Ditto by inhabitants   —   261,240

           Total quintals taken   645,322

The quintals of fish carried to fo-
   reign market   —   580,204
The tons of oil exported   —   2,846
The tierces of salmon exported   1,248

The Newfoundland fishery has at all times received, because it always merited, much of the national care. But, in extending encouragement to
that most useful class of subjects, the preference ought
surely to be given to those of the fishing and trading vessels; to the bye-boat-keepers; to the fishers,
who go yearly from Britain and Ireland, in opposition to those who reside and carry on a sedentary
fishing: For, if the use of a nursery is to supply
the public with sailors, when the dangers of war
require their aid, it is in vain to breed seamen,

K   whose

whofe fervices cannot eafily be commanded when they are wanted the moft. Ufeful regulations ought to be preferred to pecuniary bounties. And no encouragement can preferve the fifhery if a fpeedy fale is not found for the fifh, when it is cured. From the Independence of the United States we have regained a confiderable market, which the wifdom of our Councils may eafily regulate and preferve, for our own fifhers alone.

Thefe interefting truths, at leaft to a nation of iflanders, will ftill more plainly appear, from the following details :

FISH, *dried and pickled.*

	Exported from Newfoundland, Nova Scotia, and Canada.				Exported from the now United States.			
	To Britain and Ireland.	To South of Europe, Azores, &c.	To West-Indies, British and foreign.	Total.	To Britain and Ireland	To South of Europe, Azores, &c.	To West-Indies, British and foreign.	Total.
	Quintals.	Quintals.	Quintals.	Quintals.	Quintals.	Quintals.	Quintals.	Quintals.
In 1771	17,481	604,995	18,426	640,902	2,000	131,882	197,993	331,875
72	19,802	365,306	35,447	420,555	0	105,406	256,284	361,690
73	32,768	561,749	33,728	628,245	118	70,517	271,684	342,319
	Barrels.	Barrels.	Barrels.	Barrels.	Barrels.	Barrels.	Barrels.	Barrels.
In 1771	395	599	458	1,452	4	259	41,011	41,274
72	326	393	548	1,267	24	488	29,795	30,305
73	361	907	647	1,915	2	155	37,603	37,760

But this statement will not be admitted to be a genuine account of the relative importance of the British and American fishery, by those who know, that the New Englanders purchased much of their fish at Newfoundland, which they afterwards exported to foreign markets. And a comparative view of both those fisheries is subjoined, in order to shew more distinctly, which of them forms the great mart, whence the British West-Indies may be amply supplied.

| Fish exported from Newfoundland, Canada, and Nova Scotia. | Fish exported from the now United States. |

Fish exported from Newfoundland, Canada, and Nova Scotia.

Quintals.

In 1771—To Britain and Ireland   17,481
South of Europe, &c.   604,975
West-Indies, British and foreign — 18,426

640,902

Add the fish bought by the New English at Newfoundland, which appears from the Custom-house entry to have been imported Coastways   67,012

Whole produce of the now British fishery — 707,914

Fish exported from the now United States.

Quintals.

In 1771—To Britain and Ireland   2,000
To South of Europe, &c.   131,882
To West-Indies, British and foreign — 330,875

330,875

Deduct the fish bought by the New English at Newfoundland and afterwards exported from their own ports   67,012

Whence we perceive, the whole produce of the American fishery to have only been — 263,863

Thus, we see, that the revolted Colonies had engroffed almoft the whole of the Weft-India markets. And thus we perceive from what fource the Britifh Weft-Indies may be moft amply fupplied with fifh, when we confider, that their whole confumption amounted only, to about 161,000 quintals of dried and 16,178 barrels of pickled fifh, if we may judge from an average of three years importation, ending with 1773; and when we reflect too, that the general price at Newfoundland was feven fhillings the quintal, while it was ufually nine at Bofton.

That we enjoyed a confiderable fifhery not only at Newfoundland, but alfo on the American coafts, before New England was planted, is a melancholy truth, which we know from the debates in Parliament, during the year 1621, if Sir Jofiah Child had not recorded the fact, during the reign of Charles II. and lamented the impolicy of permiting it. The American charters, which were granted by Charles I. are all remarkable for a cautious claufe, referving to the refidents of England and Ireland the right of fifhing in the bays and harbours of the Colonies and drying the fifh on their lands. The ardent people, who formed the fettlement of New England were foon driven by their neceffities to begin the labours of the fifher. The hardy inhabitants of the Weftern Coafts of England, who ufed annually to refort to the American fhores, found too powerful competitors in the planters, who had emigrated from Dorfet, Devon,

and

and other Weſtern parts of England ; whoſe ſu-
perior advantages in their new ſituation, converted
ere long an annual fiſhery from England into a ſta-
tionary one, at the diſtance of three thouſand
miles. With a ſimilar ſpirit the New Englanders
engaged in the fiſheries of Newfoundland, though
not with the ſame excluſive ſucceſs. And in proportion as that enterpriſing people became competitors with the fiſhers of Britain, during her
civil and foreign wars, their rivalry narrowed the
nurſery, which had been deſtined to furniſh the
Britiſh navy with a hardy race. For, the American
ſeamen, like the Britiſh, could not be preſſed into
the public ſervice, ſince they were exempted, not ſo
much by act of Parliament *, as by the ſpirit of the
country.

Owing to thoſe unhappy cauſes Newfoundland
had long ceaſed to have much direct trade with the
Britiſh Weſt Indies. If we may determine from
an average of the years 1771--2--3 there were directly ſent to that market of the Fiſh of Newfoundland no more than 3922 quintals, 769 hogſheads,
and 67 barrels. The New Englanders almoſt en-
tirely ſupplied the fiſheries of Newfoundland with
molaſſes, ſugars, and other products of the Weſt
Indies, with immenſe quantities of rum, from their
own diſtilleries. In return they carried off the
products of the fiſhery, into their own ports, a con-
ſiderable quantity of that inferior and frugal quality, which was ſuitable to the iſlands for whoſe
consumption

* 6 Ann. ch. 37. ſec. 9.

confumption the fmall and broken fifh were culled.
Of this gainful bufinefs the revolt deprived the Americans, with other greater benefits. And during
the war a direct traffic, between Newfoundland and
the Britifh Weft Indies, was opened, which proved
equally advantageous to both. A market was even
found for the refufe fifh in the free ports of the foreign iflands. And thus, what the Americans loft,
in purfuit of their object, Britifh fubjects have
gained and may keep, unlefs we reject the favours,
which fortune has thrown in our way.

Scotland is faid to have enjoyed a confiderable
fifhery in ancient times. It did not however defcend
to the epoch of the union; which was dreaded and
oppofed by the Dutch*; becaufe their commercial
jealoufy fufpected, that the wealth of England
would be employed, in urging the Scotch to refume
and regain the fifheries, which their misfortunes,
or evil habits had loft. What the Dutch thus
forefaw and feared actually happened in time.
The Parliament wifely gave a bounty, in 1750, of
thirty fhillings a ton, on fuch buffes as fhould be
employed in the white herring fifhery, under fpecific qualifications. Before the year 1768, the Parliamentary bounty had created 263 buffes, carrying
12.556 tons, which were navigated by 2,898 men,
who caught 28,162 barrels of herrings †. It was
probably from a fifhery, thus created by a wife
measure,

* As we know from a memorial of Doctor D'Avenant to
Lord Godolphin, in the Paper-office.
† A detail from the Cuftom-houfe.

meaſure, which ought alone to evince to the United States what the wealth of Britain can do, when employed on her own improvement, that Scotland exported to the Weſt Indies of HERRINGS ;

In 1767	—	8,273 Barrels
In 1768	—	10,830
In 1769	—	8,435 ;

beſides tuſk, ling and ſalmon, in much ſmaller quantities. The amount had perhaps been greater had the competition of the revolted Colonies been leſs. When that competition was removed, by the war, England alone ſent ſupplies of pickled fiſh to the Britiſh Weſt Indies nearly equal to the conſumption, as we have already evinced. The Britiſh fiſh fetch a higher price than the American, becauſe they are of higher reliſh and more capable of preſervation. The extenſion of circumjacent fiſheries and the improvement of internal waſtes are the only objects, which greatly merit the bounties of the Britiſh nation ; owing to the nature of its defence and frequency of attack. But, the beſt bounty, becauſe the cheapeſt and moſt ſuccesſful, is the opening and extending of markets, wherein there ſhall be no competitors. Whether the Britiſh fiſheries, European and American, can ſupply the Britiſh Weſt-Indies with 161,000 quintals of dried and 16,200 barrels of pickled fiſh ; whether that cargo ought to be ſupplied by Britiſh ſubjects, excluſive of American citizens ; are queſ-

L   tions,

tions, which he would be idle, who fhould fit down to anfwer.

It will be found perhaps much more difficult to procure for the Weft Indies an adequate fupply of live provifions and live flock, which the proclamation properly allowed to be fent them from the United States, if the American governments fhould, in their anger, prohibit the export in *Britifh* fhips. The neceffary cargo is not a fmall one; as we may learn from the following detail :

LIVE STOCK,

Exported from the now United States to the Britifh Weft Indies,

		Horfes, No.	Cattle, No.	Sheep and Hogs, No.	Poultry, dozen.
In	1771,	2170	1148	4812	1007
	72,	2220	1296	3693	939
	73,	2768	1203	5320	799

Yet, the numbers of each kind are not beyond the poffibility of accommodation from the Britifh dominions. Horfes, we know, have been fent to the Weft Indies from Britain and Ireland, during every age, in proportion probably, as they were not excluded by the competition of the revolted Colonies. Since the epoch of Independence low priced horfes have been actually exported from Scotland. In the two and twenty years, ending with 1771, there were exported from England to every country, no fewer than 29,131 horfes *. There feems then no reafon to doubt, but the bogs of Ireland,

the

* See the Annual Regifter, 1773.

the mountains of Scotland, and the heaths of Cornwall, will produce garrons enow to answer the full demand of four and twenty hundred, without prostituting the hunters of Yorkshire to the drudgery of the mill. From the peace of 1763 Canada supplied the Southern settlements with many serviceable horses, by the route of Lake Champlain, which were sometimes exported to the West Indies; but Canada sent none by the River St. Laurence: The channel of the Champlain being now obstructed the surplus number will assuredly form a part of the mixed cargoes, which will now be sent directly to the British West Indies, in prosecution of a more vigorous commerce. The forests of Nova Scotia have hitherto bred few horses. When the energy of the new settlers shall have banked out the tide, we may reasonably expect, that their meadows will raise horses sufficient to supply even the wants of neighbours, from their Eastern harbours, which, stretching far into the ocean, court the traffick of every country.

The fields, which, from their herbage, produce horses, will equally rear cattle of every other kind. Canada and Nova Scotia have not yet supplied the West Indies with any number of oxen. Commerce, like every thing else, must have its beginning and its end. Virginia and New England were originally stocked with the ox and the sheep from England. Both however gained from her in less than forty years the supply of the West Indies, which they, with the other revolted colonies, chiefly enjoyed

L 2

joyed

joyed previous to the late civil war. Canada and
Nova Scotia have yet to learn how to form that
mifcellaneous cargo, confifting of provifions alive
and falted, of lumber, and of almoft every thing,
which the neceffities, rather than the elegancies of
life require. Till both have acquired the pedling
arts of their neighbours, (and it were to be wifhed
that every part of the Britifh dominions would prac-
tife a pedling more than a magnificent commerce,)
Ireland alone can fupply from her moft luxuriant
paftures the full demand of cattle for the Weft India market, fince Ireland anually exported, according to an average of feven years, ending with 1777,
four thoufand and forty live flock exclufive of
hogs *. From the coaft of Barbary the Weft Indies were often fupplied with fheep; and from the
Cape de Verd Iflands they were fometimes furnifhed with cattle and Indian corn. It is of greater
nautical importance to Britain, to fend fheep and
oxen to the Weft Indies, from the Barbary Coaft
and the Cape de Verd's, than from Nova Scotia
or Canada ; becaufe the chief care of Britain, on
this occafion, fhould be, to find outward freights
for the Weft India veffels, confifting of fix hundred and eighty fail ; to make that bufinefs profitable now, which was formerly unprofitable, owing,
to the greater bulk of the homeward than the outward ladings : And in this meafure all parties are
equally interefted, becaufe if fhips are fully freight-
ed

---

* Appendix to Mr. A. Young's Tour in Ireland, which
contains many interefting details.

ed to the West Indies they can transport the West
India products the cheaper to Britain. Lastly;
if the West Indians shall continue too high-minded
to raise their own poultry, they may find feeders in
Bermudas : And Bermudas alone can send them
all the poultry, which their luxuries may crave,
since the Bermudeans sent them 741 dozen, in
1772, as part of an accustomed cargo *.

If from the offspring of pasturage we turn our
attention to the products of agriculture we shall
find the flour of wheat to have been an article,
which the West Indians consumed in considerable
quantities, though their slaves were seldom allowed to taste it.

Of Flour and Bread
there were exported to the British West Indies ;
In 1771, — 136,388 barrels, 4,515 kegs
72, — 126,229 — 4,960
73, — 134,638 — 3,624.

If the United States should refuse their former
supplies, the considerable quantity †, which was
thus consumed in the British West Indies, must be
collected from various sources. Nova Scotia has
hitherto had no surplus of flour or of wheat to
spare. The agriculture of Canada was, for several
years after the conquest, overshadowed by the superior advantages of the middle colonies. It was
the cheapness of the Canadian wheat, owing to
the absence of buyers, which induced the Phila-
delphian

* The Inspector's Books.

† Id.

delphian merchants to become speculators in the market of Quebec, for supplying directly the demands of Portugal and Spain. And Canada actually exported *

	Bushels wheat.	Barrels of flour.
In 1772,	154,807	720
73,	264,916	7,091
74,	460,818	6,991
75,	175,059	7,115
78,	14,175	20,521

The Canadians, like their Southern neighbours, have acquired an energy from the war, which, like them, they will carry into all the operations of peace. To argue, that the Canadians, because they were once indolent and poor, are never to become active and opulent, is to insist that the affairs of the world do not run continually in a progress; that children never become men; that every people have not their beginning, their rise, and their decline. The historian will find no great difficulty, in pointing out the exact period, when each of the revolted Colonies exported a less quantity of wheat and flour than Canada actually sent out, as its surplus, in 1772. When the United States, in their spirit of resentment, rather than retaliation, shall have withdrawn the competition of their citizens; when a constant demand shall have operated as an encouragement to the manufacturing of wheat; then will Canada supply both Newfoundland and the British West Indies with a sufficient quantity of flour, which when well packed keeps

* Inspect. Gen. Books.

keeps for years. The frofts of Canada, the ftorms
of St. Lawrence, the foggs of Nova Scotia, have all
been mentioned triumphantly as natural infelicities,
which muft for ever prevent Canada and Nova
Scotia from becoming confiderable, in agriculture,
or great in trade. The mildnefs of the laft winter
in Nova Scotia, while the rivers and bays of the
United States, as far as Carolina, continued frozen
till the beginning of March, ought to moderate
that triumph in future. The fame North-Weft
wind, which renders it fo difficult for veffels to
afcend the St. Lawrence after the middle of
October, facilitates the navigation outwards. And
Halifax might eafily be converted into a depofitory
for all the furplus products of Nova Scotia and
Canada; which might afterwards be fent out, during every feafon, as demand required, from that
moft commodious of all the American harbours.
Halifax is faid to be the moft commodious port, becaufe it is not only at all times open, but it happily
ftretches about five degrees to the Eaftward of
Chefapeake Bay; the North-Weft wind, which
drives with irrefiftable violence fo many fhips from
the coafts of the United States, carries them fafely
to Halifax, by a fide-long preffure; and the Gulf
ftream conveys every veffel from the South, during
the calmer weather, by an eafy fail along the
American fhores to this moft fecure retreat.

Whatever productions, the ploughs of Canada,
or Nova Scotia, may ever afford, Great Britain
will furely be able to furnifh all the flour of wheat,

which

which the Britiſh Weſt Indies can ever require, if from our experience we may form any expectation. Even young men may remember ſince England ſupplied the coaſts of the Mediterranean; as well as the ſhores of the Baltic, with wheat. During that flouriſhing period of our agriculture, from 1740 to 1757, England exported annually-* about 750,000 quarters of corn, which at the low prices of that time, brought into the nation £.1,300,000. Such plenty alas! and ſuch profit from Corn we have not for ſome years known. However unfavourable the ſeaſons may prove there is reaſon to hope, from the flouriſhing ſtate of our agriculture, that Great-Britain will be able to ſpare wheat flour enough to ſupply the wants of a community of ſeventy thouſand maſters. For, there were actually exported to the Britiſh Weſt-Indies from England alone :

	Wheat flour.	Oatmeal.	Bread.
	Quarters.	Quarters.	Cwt.
In 1773 —	0 —	18 —	404
1780 —	35,907 —	758 —	32,587
1783 —	4,090 —	125 —	6,657

The quarter of meal muſt weigh 276lbs: So we may regard every quarter as only a greater barrel. From theſe Cuſtom-houſe entries, with all their imperfections, we ſee clearly enough the effect

* An. Reg. 1772.

effect of the American competition when it exifted, and when it had ceafed. Whatever may be the fyftem which the Parliament fhall adopt, with regard to corn, it will be wife to continue, the allowance, which has for fome years been given *, to export grain and other provifions to the Britifh Weft-Indies, like the indulgence that has ufually been granted to Man, Guernfey, and Jerfey. We are very apt to copy the French fafhions while we too feldom adopt the French policy. What the French practice even now is, we may learn from the edict of the Vifcount de Damas, in July 1783, which has been lately cited as fo favourable to the United States; and which yet permits— " Their merchants to furnifh our Colonies (of France) with every kind of their commodities, *that our nation cannot fupply us with*." We ought not to hefitate a moment then, in recuring to the original principle of colonization, which confifted, in fupplying all that the Plantations might want and that Britain could furnifh, exclufive of every other country. And thus we perceive, how much favour the Congrefs would confer upon Britain, were that body to prohibit the export of flour to the Britifh Weft-Indies ; how much benefit Britain conferred on the American citizens, when fhe allowed flour to be exported from the United States to the Britifh Weft-Indies in *Britifh* fhips.

M   It

---

* By 23 Geo. III. ch. 6. this allowance was continued to the 1ft of May 1784.

It will be much more difficult to find for the West Indies a sufficient supply of rice and Indian corn, which are both said to be absolutely essential. It is however a comfortable consideration, that neither rice nor Indian corn formed the food of the slaves. Of rice there were only imported in the British West Indies, if we may judge from a three years average ending with 1773, 20563 barrels *, which were all consumed at the luxurious tables of the seventy thousand masters. Of Indian corn there were equally required, if we may determine from a similar average, 401,471 bushels † ; which had done something more than furnish 400,000 slaves with one week's supply, had the negroes consumed what was actually given to the horses and other labouring cattle. Rice then was a luxury of the rich ; and Indian corn was the food of labourers, who indeed were equally entitled to their hire. It is not then so much to be lamented, that from the United States, rice and Indian corn can alone be procured in sufficient quantities. But, every

community

---

* The Custom-house entries.

† Id. Indian corn was the only article of provisions, which was unreasonable in its price, according to the latest accounts from the West-Indies. It was as high as 5s. 10d. sterling per bushel at Antigua in April : But, it was about the same time as high as 4s. sterling the bushel in Virginia ; and corn was selling in the Baltimore market on the 18 of May 1784 at 3s. sterling the bushel. All these high prices were owing to the severity of the preceding winter, when the planters were obliged to feed their cattle with the corn which they used to export.

community, which thus depends on rivals, ought to look for fubftitutes when they can no longer find fupplies. Every houfe-wife can find a thoufand fubftitutes for rice, in the making of her puddings: And peafe, beans, oats and barley, we know feed the horfes of other countries. The oats, which were raifed in the United States, were of a kind too light, and the peafe were too fub- ject to the ravages of the fly to afford much food: And oats and beans were chiefly fupplied from Britain even before the revolt put an end to the colonial competition. From England alone there were actually fent to the Britifh Weft-Indies;

	Barley. qrs.	Peafe. qrs.	Beans. qrs.	Oats. qrs.	Wheat. qrs.	Rye. qrs.
In 1773	3	356	9,089	16,615	0	350
In 1780	256	1,116	12,291	8,006	1,146	1,116
In 1783	146	755	7,360	6,129	8	755

From thefe Cuftom-houfe entries we fee clearly, by contrafting the exports of the three years, the effect of competition between Great Britain and the United States. The revolted Colonies had gra- dually circumvented the Parent Country, in fup- plying the Britifh Weft Indies, with all the pro- ductions of agriculture. The Britifh yeomanry, burdened with the payment of rents, tythes, and poor-rates, could not contend with the American yeomanry, who were exempted from all thefe taxes, befides much lighter public duties. And Mr. Arthur Young very ably proved, in 1774, by

an

an examination of particulars *, that the American
farmer could not only fupply the Weft-India market with flour, much cheaper than the Englifh
farmer could do ; but, could even exclude the
Englifh farmer from fupplying the domeftic markets of Britain with wheat. It is curious to remark how near to each other the events of the late
war have brought the prices of provifions in America and in Britain. The current rates at the two
great marts of Philadelphia and London, in December 1783, may be compared, by the following
detail :

	Philadelphia prices.			London prices.		
Of fine flour per cwt.	£. 0	15	9	£. 0	16	0
Of common ditto	0	13	0	0	14	0
Of mefs beef per barrel	2	2	6	2	2	6
Of mefs pork	3	0	0	2	8	0
	£.6	11	3	£.6	0	6

It is a remarkable fact, that the prices of all
things have been uncommonly high in the United
States, fince the peace. Yet it is apparent that the
London and Philadelphia prices cannot thus run
parallel together long † ; though the freights may
continue cheaper from London than from Philadelphia. The advantages of the American farmer,
notwithftanding the additional burdens of independence,

* Political Arithmetic.

† The fubjoined detail will evince the truth of the pofition
in the text, that the American prices of grain are already
fallen

dence, will continue fo fuperior, in refpect to rents, tythes, and poor-rates, over the Britifh farmer, that the former muft ere long overpower the latter in every competition. The difference of price to the Weft Indians, whatever it may be, is the equivalent, which they ought to pay to the Britifh confumer for enjoying the exclufive fupply of fugar rum and other Weft India products. But, the American citizens having now ceafed to be fellow-fubjects, may be juftly excluded from a right and a benefit, which we had formerly relinquifhed in favour to them. The Britifh farmers next to the Britifh failors are the men, who are the moft worthy of the protection of the Britifh legiflature : The one clafs fights our battles ; the other fupplies us with food : The farmers are therefore entitled to the preference in fupplying the Weft India markets with all the productions of agriculture : The failors are ftill more entitled to the employment,

fallen much lower than the Britifh, and will probably continue fo :

	At London, 18th May, 1784.	At Baltimore, the mart of the middle States, 18th May, 1784.
Wheat —	£.2 8 1 per qr. —	£.1 12 0 per qr.
Peafe —	1 13 2 ditto. —	1 4 0 ditto.
Beans —	1 8 6 ditto. —	1 4 0 ditto.
Barley —	1 6 9 ditto. —	0 16 9 ditto.
Oats —	1 0 5 ditto. —	0 8 8 ditto.

Yet, falted provifions were at the fame time much higher in the Baltimore market, than in the London.

ment, which arises from additional freights. And the public will gain in the exact proportion, as the interest of those two most useful bodies of men are promoted.

The West Indians however, like every other people, ought to be chiefly supplied with ground provisions, by their own diligence and care. Let every island follow the example of the Jamaica Assembly when it enacted *: " That owners of plantations shall have at all times one acre of ground well planted with provisions for every five negroes, and so proportionably, under the penalty of forty shillings, for every acre wanting." The law has long expired; but the salutariness of the rule has in a good measure continued the practice: And Jamaica, considering its superior extent and populousness, of all the West-India islands, requires the smallest supply of provisions from abroad. Virginia and Maryland are the States, which chiefly supplied the West Indies with corn: Yet, during almost a century, after the successive settlement of each, their Assemblies constantly enforced by penalties the planting of grain in opposition to tobacco †. The planters of both at length discovered, that on the

* Laws 1684.

† The laws of Virginia, which was settled in 1607, directed in 1663: That two acres of corn should be yearly planted for each tythable, tending a crop; and that the planting of one acre of wheat should excuse the planting of two acres of corn: [Laws p. 42.] And considerable encouragement was given to the building of water-mills in 1705. (Laws p. 294.] land Marypassed similar laws, 1682 ch. 1. 1705 ch. 16.

the fame plantation, with the fame number of
negroes, they could raife a crop of wheat, in addition to the ufual crop of tobacco. And the Weft
Indians ought to adopt the principle and profit
from the refult of this difcovery; which alone confifts, in making the beft ufe of their advantages.
Without the law of Jamaica the other iflands had
been driven by neceffity to adopt the practice, of
raifing on their own fields much ground provifions.
And this policy is fo ufeful to the mafter and agreeable to the flave, that it ought to be extended and
enforced by the Weft India Legiflatures: This
rural œconomy is ufeful to the mafter, becaufe
money faved is money gained, which depends on
no contingencies: It is pleafant to the flave, becaufe, while he labours his own field, and tends
his own plantains, potatoes and yams, he thinks he
is free. Why then fhould the Weft Indians refift
a meafure, which promifes profit to themfelves and
happinefs to others?

Yet, the Weft India merchants and planters reprefented to the King's Minifters in April 1783:
" That in feveral of his Majefty's Sugar Colonies
there are ftill great tracts of uncultivated lands, of
which although a confiderable part would undoubtedly under adequate encouragement be fettled
with fugar works, yet there will remain confiderable quantities, which from foil or fituation are
unfit for the culture of fugar, though very fit for
that of indigo, coffee, cocoa and tobacco, if proper
encouragement were given thereto." And the encouragement

couragement thus anxiously asked by them is the distribution of bounties from the taxes of Britain, which are collected from our industrious classes. They ought to be told, that we wish not so much for their indigo and coffee, their cocoa and tobacco, as that they would, instead thereof, raise food for their slaves. Let their Assemblies encourage by bounties, or enforce by penalties, the raising of the most needful kind of provisions on their own islands. Let them adopt every possible mode of supply rather than be dependent on rivals, or by sacrificing the acts of navigation, enervate the best defence of Britain, who lately protected them from conquest.

2. Having thus shewn, that it is possible to supply the British West-Indies with provisions exclusive of the United States; that it is the interest of Britain to supply them exclusive of the United States; it is now proper to advert secondly to the commerce of lumber, which the necessities of the builder and cooper require. The present demand is great; as we may learn from the following detail of the former supply:

There were exported from the United States to the British West-Indies in 1771;

Pine and oak boards, planks, lathing, &c. — }	21,271,955 feet
Hoops — —	1,958,411 numb.
Staves and heading —	7,200,000 numb.
Pine timber — —	200 tons
Oak timber — —	95 tons

Exclufive of fmaller articles this cargo was certainly of a bulk, which required many fhips to
carry it: And without the aid of the United States
it will not be eafy to find an adequate fupply for
fo large a demand. Canada and Nova Scotia, for
fome years before the revolt, had furnifhed the
Britifh Weft-Indies with fome lumber of the various kinds. Both thefe colonies had however
been depreffed by too powerful competitors and
both continued feeble; the one from its paucity
of people; the other from the inveteracy of its
habits: And both wanted what it is of the greateft
confequence for every community to poffefs, *energy*
and *capital*. The face of both countries, however
extenfive, is luxuriantly covered with timber trees,
and both are every where interfected by navigable
rivers: In Canada the people had before the
revolt erected great numbers of faw-mills of a
cheap and commodious conftruction: In Nova
Scotia it is hoped the fettlers, by following now
their example will ere long convert their extenfive
forefts into fruitful fields. Canada has been lately
confined within narrower bounds, which will reftrain the accuftomed roving of its woodfmen;
who as they encreafe in numbers will want employment; and who will therefore direct their
future diligence to domeftic occupations with the
force, which compreffion always produces. The
extenfive fhores of the Bay of Fundy (where the
proper wood for lumber abounds with even the
white oak, fo prized for its clofenefs of grain) have

been

been at length settled by a great body of men; from whose energy of character and knowledge of the business, scantlings for the builder and staves for the cooper may be expected in abundance, as they convert the well-earned rewards of their loyalty into productive farms. Nor, could the same quantity of products be expected indeed from the twenty-six thousand people, who inhabited Nova Scotia before the late war, as from the superior industry and wealth of the sixty-six thousand fishers and farmers, who now reside in that flourishing province. If the Congress, incited by the clamours of interested traders, should prohibit the export of lumber to the British West-Indies, the prohibition would operate as a bounty to Canada and Nova Scotia, by clearing the markets of overpowering competitors and creating a demand, which, owing chiefly to that competition, they were unable to supply. But, the planters, who appoint the American Legislatures, are too much benefitted from finding a market for the timber, which lies heavy on their lands, to give us any well grounded reason to hope, for a measure so peculiarly advantageous to the British dominions.

If however, resentment should in the struggle prove too powerful for prudence, and contrary to their genuine interests the United States should prohibit the export of lumber to the British West-Indies, it will be proper to look for adequate supplies from every quarter of the globe. The search would not be difficult were the real advantage of Britain the

point

point to be fimply confidered. And the nava,
policy of Britain requires, that the Britifh Weft-
Indies fhould be fupplied with lumber from the
rivers of Germany and the fhores of the Baltic,
even in preference to Canada and to Nova Scotia.
For, it was the opinion of Sir Jofiah Child, which
the experience of a century hath verified;" That
there is nothing more prejudicial and in profpect
more dangerous to any mother kingdom than the
encreafe of fhipping in their plantations and provinces:" And from the regifter of fhipping at
Lloyd's Coffee-houfe we may learn, that the Colonifts have begun to build fhips in Nova Scotia
and Canada and that the Britifh merchants have
conftructed, fince the revolt, veffels of three
hundred tons at Newfoundland and fmaller ones on
the inhofpitable fhores of Labradore. Whether
the nautical interefts of the kingdom would be promoted the moft, by the building of fhips at Poole,
(fince it is the merchants at Poole who chiefly build
fhips at Newfoundland and Labradore) or at Newfoundland, is a queftion which does not merit any
anfwer: Nor, is it neceffary to enquire, whether
Britain would be moft benefitted, by fetching the
wood from Newfoundland, or by fending thither
the iron and fails: And thus it is, fays Montefquieu, that Holland has its quarries and its forefts.

In this manner are we led to infer, that neither
the petty profits of the Weft-Indians, who enjoy
monopolies enow, nor a confiderable advantage to
our remaining colonifts, who may convert their

trees

trees into potafh, ought to be confidered a moment, when the domeftic encreafe of fhipwrights,
failors, and coopers, is the objeét in contemplation.
The colonies were originally fettled to promote
the navigation of England, by creating a great
employment for fhips. To allow the plantations
(as they have been allowed for a century and a
half) to enter into a competition with the mother
country, in fhip-building and navigation, was abfurdly to facrifice the important end to the inconfiderable means. The fifheries of New-England
were, in this view of the fubjeét, a nuifance in the
Britifh empire, great in proportion to their extent
and continuance. The making of aéts of Parliament
to proteét the New-England fifhers and the colonial failors from being preffed into the public fervice, like other Britifh fifhers and feamen, was to
augment that nuifance, inftead of abetting it.—
Sailors, who refide at a diftance of three thoufand
miles, were they fubjeét to the prefs, are unufeful
to Britain, becaufe their fervices cannot be commanded, when they are wanted moft. The failors
and fifhers of Nova Scotia and Canada are entitled
therefore to no favour from Britain. And ftill
lefs are the American feamen, who continue our
rivals in peace, and will be our enemies in war,
entitled to any indulgence, when that favour is to be
conferred by depriving our own failors of employment, and the nation confequently of their fervice.
When the Weft-Indians are urged to allow their
flaves to raife food for themfelves they conftantly
plead,

plead, that the planting of fugar promotes the navigation of Britain. But, when they infift, that the American citizens fhall be allowed to fupply them with lumber in *American fhips*, even of the fmalleft fize, they would facrifice the *end* to the *means*. And the Weft Indians little reflect, amid their cares for themfelves, that in proportion as they carry their wifhes into effect they deftroy the ufefulnefs of the Weft Indies to Britain.

It ought to be the conftant object of Britain then, confidering her glory and defence to arife chiefly from her fhips and her failors, to ranfack the earth for lumber and to fupply the Weft Inpies from her own ports. Were this meafure carried carefully into practice it would be found to lead to the profit of individuals as well as to the fafety of the State. The navigation, which was created, by tranfporting annually the furplus products of the Weft Indies to Britain, is doubtlefs of great importance, from its magnitude, and may be rendered much more ufeful, by its regulation. This truth we fhall fee in the moft ftriking light by attentively viewing the fubjoined detail of the Weft-India fhipping, which was formed from a minute infpection of the entries at the Cuftom-houfe *:

And

---

* Some men from the fuggeftions of fceptical minds delight in all the various fhades of uncertainty. Such men are never more gratified than in finding errors in the Cuftom-houfe books, becaufe the eftablifhment of error has an effential tendency to create univerfal doubt. But, in thofe books there is affuredly much truth as well as fome falfehood : The entries

of

And it contains an accurate abstract of the number of vessels, which appears from the registers of shipping to have been cleared from each respective island, during a year of great export, distinguishing the British from American built shipping :

Islands.	Brit. Ships.	Am. ships.	Brit. tons.	Am. tons.
Jamaica	145—136 —	26,906 —	15,847
Barbadoes -	47 — 13 —	6,546 —	1,172
St. Kitt's -	35 — 20 —	6,494 —	2,310
Antigua -	28 — 22 —	4,073 —	2,290
St. Vincent's	25 — 9 —	3,042 —	1,100
Tobago -	6 — 3 —	615 —	320
Montserrat -	10 — 9 —	1,437 —	1,043
Nevis - -	18 — 0 —	2,851 —	
Grenades -	51 — 49 —	7,717 —	5,942
Dominica -	32 — 21 —	3,933 —	2,433
British -	397 - - -	63,614.	
American -	282 - - -	32,457.	
Tot. in 1772, -	679 - - -	96,071	

From this detail, which is only instructive in proportion to its accuracy, and which to be able

thus

of uncustomed goods are doubtless liable to much imposition, and are consequently obnoxious to much objection, as proofs. The entries of the number of ships, which clear in any port in any year, contain as much certainty as generally is found in human affairs. Every vessel, which any where loads and all the vessels which loaded in the West-India islands, during any given year, must have necessarily cleared, and every ves-

sel

thus to submit to the Public required no small re-
search, we may make many reflections. From it
we see the relative importance of each of those
islands to our navigation and the commercial magnitude of the whole. Tobago indeed we have
lost ; but, it was the least we could loose. Of the
six hundred and seventy-nine vessels, which were
in this manner required to transport the great West
India cargo of 1772 to Britain, much more than
two thirds had been built in our Colonies, though
they only contained a little more than one half of
the tonnage. To so great an extent had we resigned
the most useful of all our manufactures to our Colonists, contrary to the remonstrances of the wisest
men of their time. We have been sufficiently soli-
citous about the manufactures of wool, of hats, and
of iron in the Colonies; but we have cared little,
during the last century, for the more important
manufacture of ships. This had been a melancholy remark, were it not that we may derive
consolation from reflecting, how much the public
wisdom may convert misfortunes into benefits. We

may

fel is entered accordingly to the description given of her
in her own register; namely *where she was built and who
are her owners*. In this transaction interest has no object in
propagating falsehood. And consequently when the Custom-
house lists of all vessels, which entered outwards in any year
from the British West-Indies, are carefully inspected, we gain
all the certainty which, in such details, any reasonable inquirer
would wish to have. In this manner were the West India
Custom-house returns inspected by two very competent persons, in order to come at the result mentioned in the text.

may now regain the bufinefs of fhip building to no fmall extent, which our imprudent kindnefs had given away : Our fafety requires, that we ought to retain every advantage, which a fignal revolution has happily thrown in our way.

Of thofe fix hundred and feventy nine veffels, which though regiftered at ninety-fix thoufand tons, carried at leaft one hundred and twenty eight tons, it is admitted, that one half failed to the Weft Indies without a freight, or that each fhip carried only half a lading. The lofs from that circumftance formerly and the gain to be made now, by finding full freights for our outward-bound fhips, may be very eafily calculated. If the average of the outward freights is allowed to be twelve and fix pence the ton, we may find by an eafy calculation, that the freights on fixty-four thoufand tons would amount to forty thoufand pounds. To men indeed who permit their minds to dwell on fplendid projects of commerce, or who gain thoufands from a job, that annual gain to an opulent nation will appear very inconfiderable. But it is the duty of the Legiflature of a nation, who runs too much into a magnificent trade, to promote an œconomical one. If that employment of capital, which was formerly unproductive, can be rendered, by proper meafures, more fruitful, we may furely prefume, that an augmentation of capital would neceffarily follow additional gains. Merchants, who formerly became owners of fhips in the Weft India trade with reluctance, would now purchafe fhares with alacrity.

The

The number of veſſels would increaſe with the competition of traders. And in this manner would Great Britain, by ſupplying the Weſt Indies with Lumber from her own ports, regain the building of ſhips and invigorate that branch of her navigation, which the continued competition of her Colonies for upwards of a century had bowed down and broken.

But to the moſt ſalutary meaſure objections may be eaſily found at the call of intereſt. "If it were poſſible, ſay the Weſt Indian Committee, to confine the intercourſe between the Sugar Colonies and America to Britiſh built ſhips, is it quite ſo clear, as men imagine, that we have ſhips to carry it on, or can keep up ſuch a ſtock of Britiſh ſhipping in the merchants ſhips, as would be wanted ?" Conſidering this queſtion as an important one (and an important one it ſurely is) thoſe gentlemen do not rely on general reaſoning, but appeal to the deciſive inferences of authentic facts. In purſuance of their plan they have brought before the Public the regiſter of ſhipping, which are conſtantly ſurveyed and weekly tranſmitted for the uſe of that very reſpectable body of men, the Inſurers at Lloyd's Coffee-houſe. This regiſter, containing a return of the name of every ſhip, its tonnage and age, *the place where built*, the owner, the uſual trade, wherein employed, with other more minute particulars of its quality, is very uſeful to them : And comprehending, as it does, almoſt all the ſhips, which are employed in the *foreign* trade of Britain, it furniſhes a very good comparative eſtimate of the num-

O   ber

ber and nature of our shipping, at any two given epochs, within the last six and twenty years, the period of its existance. The Committee, by using the register of 1775, which comprehends the reports of 1772--3--4 and part of 1775, chose the æra of the greatest extent of navigation, which had ever transported the surplus products of England. For, from the register of shipping at the Customhouse, we know, that, according to a three years average ending with 1751, which was an age of commercial prosperity beyond former example, there were cleared outwards only ;

	Tons Eng.	Tons For.	Tot. Tons.
	609,798	51,386	661,184

Yet there entered out-
wards, according to
a three years average
ending with 1774, - 756,187 - 65,630 - 821,817

It was at this epoch of nautical greatness, that the Committee thought proper to inspect the Register and to publish the result. The public had been still more obliged to them, had they ransacked the Register, since the peace and equally published their researches, that the world might have enjoyed the satisfaction of contrasting two such signal æras together. What the Committee thus declined to do has been actually done. And the Register of 1783, which contains the reports of 1781-2-3 has been examined with the most minute care; in order to form a comparison between a peaceful period of unexampled prosperity and a hostile period of uncommon embarrassments. And the following detail contains :

A COMPARATIVE

A COMPARATIVE VIEW of the Shipping, which were employed, in the *Foreign Trade* of Britain, at the Commencement and End of the late War, as they appear in the Register of the Insurers at Lloyds Coffee-house, distinguishing the British from the American built Ships.

The Shipping of 1772-3-4.

British built ships 3,908, their tonnage	605,645	
American ditto 2,311, ditto	373,618	
6,219	979,263	

The Shipping of 1781-2-3.

British built ships 3,848, their tonnage	708,346	
American ditto 1,334, ditto	225,439	
Deficience in 5,182	933,785	
1,037 and	45,478	
6,219	979,269	

It is thus apparent, that of the whole deficience of there were only wanting, in 1783, of *British* ships — 60
and of *American* ships — 977
1037 — 1037 vessels;

Yet, that the total inferiority of the period of war to the period of peace amounted only to — 102,701 British tons;
while there was an increase of — 148,179 American tons;
and a decrease of — 45,478 tons.

Such is the result of a comparison, which ought
surely to inspire no despondence even into the
most fearful minds. The West-India Committee
very well remark : " That the tonnage of both is
much below the truth, being the tonnage the ships
were registered at; that it follows, as far as this
survey extended, the American shipping in the
foreign trade of Britain amounted to a good deal
more than half as much as the British." Had they
inspected the Register of 1783, they would have
seen, what indeed was not altogether within their
plan, that the British shipping had encreased by the
exclusion of the American, during the calamities of
war, no less than 102,701 tons. Of this exhilerating prospect let us take another view. There
were assuredly vast fleets, which, though built by
British shipwrights, were not included in the sur-
veys of 1781-2-3, because they had not touched at
any British port; because they were insured by
the Government, who made use of them as transports. From the Report of the Commissioners
of Public Accounts we know, that there were employed at New York by the Quarter-master General, the Barack-master, the Commissary General,
in the four years, ending with 1780, no fewer
than 611 vessels, carrying 44,016 tons. Were this
fleet brought to the account of 1783, it would
complete the defective quantity of tonnage, though
not the defective number of ships. Many of those
vessels, or perhaps a greater number, remained till
November, 1783, to perform the melancholy service

vice of final evacuation. And all those, or many of those, have again entered into the merchants service, since that signal epoch, and properly fill the void, which the happy exclusion of the American ships had left. But, what is that puny fleet to the vast navy, which was constantly employed, during the years 1781-2-3, by the Victualing Office, by the Ordnance Office, by the Navy Office? And from an inspection of Lloyd's Register we may learn, that few of these transports could have been surveyed; because the very few transports, which appear to have been reported, consisted of those vessels, that were employed by the private contractors for various supplies. When all those, or the half of those, which had been employed by the public boards, are brought to account; who shall say, that there was any deficience in 1783?

It is nevertheless asserted, that the deficiency was not supplied by British ships; but by vessels foreign built, of which the Northern nations supplied the far greater number. If it is hereby meant to affirm, that much more has happened now, than had always happened, amid former hostilities, the witness testifies of facts, which he knows not to be true.. We have been driven by all our wars to employ foreign ships, in exact proportion to our naval embarrassments, and even to our success by land. More than one half of the commerce of England was carried on in foreign shipping, during King William's wars: For it was found

coast

impoffible to man the Navy without ftopping the coaft trade, owing to the fcarcity of feamen. We employed no great number of foreign fhips, during the long courfe of hoftilities, which enfued upon the acceffion of Queen Anne, becaufe our glories by land in fome meafure protected our fhips by fea. The Spanifh war of 1739 increafed the quantity of foreign tonnage cleared outwards from 26,000 tons, during the previous peace, to 87,000 tons, amid the fubfequent hoftilities. The French war of 1755 produced fimilar effects: The foreign tonnage rofe from 51,000 in 1750 to 73,000 in 1756-7, and to 120,000 tons in 1762. Such was the progreffive force of our navigation at the epoch of the revolt, that our fhipping continued to increafe during the three years of the American war. It was the French interpofition, which forced up the foreign tonnage, from 64,000, in 1775, to 98,000, in 1778, and to 139,000 tons, in 1779. The foreign tonnage rofe ftill higher, during the Dutch war. Entangled, as we were, by our Colonies, preffed by the French, attacked by the Spaniards, fought by the Dutch, and bullied by the armed neutrality; it is not furprizing, that our traders fought fhelter under foreign flags. But, it has been fhewn * to the conviction of reafonable men, that however our navigation and traffic may be depreffed by war, both conftantly fpring up on the return of peace with ftill greater force.

The

---

* See The Eftimate of the Comparative Strength of Britain, for the facts and the inference mentioned in the text.

The foregoing truth we might even colleſt from Lloyd's Regiſter of 1783; which evinces, that the Britiſh capital, which had created and fuſtained the vaſt ſhipping of Britain, at the epoch of the revolt, far from being leſſened, or enerved, had aſtually been augmented and ſtrengthened by the war; becauſe that capital had been productive, and merchants naturally throw their ſurplus ſtock₈ into the ſtream of commerce which, as it follows, waſhes grains of gold from its banks. How many fortunes were there in faſt made, by ſupplying the government with tranſports, and even with armed ſhips, amid the preſſures of war. Now, it is productive capital, which, with the energy of compound intereſt, produces gradually ſtill greater capitals. And it is that conſtant accumulation of capital in the hands of the induſtrious claſſes, which for a century has produced, notwithſtanding our wars, our flouriſhing agriculture, our various manufaſtures, our extenſive commerce, and vaſt navigation.

After all this elaborate enquiry, it may be properly aſked, if there could have poſſibly been *three and twenty hundred* American built veſſels engaged in the foreign trade of Britain, during the years 1772—3—4—5? There may have been indeed very ancient ſhips, that had been again and again rebuilt: And Lloyd's regiſter ſhews this to have been the faſt from the moſt accurate reports, which ſpeak of American ſhips, that had been built in

1762

1762, and even before it. The following detail,
which was carefully extracted from the records of
American built shipping, will confirm sufficiently
the notices of the register, as well as the foregoing
inferences from it.

When

An account of all such vessels as were built and *registered*, in the continental colonies, with the islands of Bahamas and Bermudas, during six years, distinguishing each year, and the top-sail vessels from the sloops and schooners:

When Registered.	Topsails.	Their Tons.	Sloops, &c.	Their Tons.	Total Vessels.	Total Tons.
In — 1768	157	19,098	329	10,354	486	29,452
69	114	11,247	336	10,213	450	21,460
70	130	11,216	385	12,982	515	24,198
71	131	14,695	347	10,580	478	25,275
72	184	19,854	373	12,569	557	32,423
73	212	24,500	426	13,529	638	38,029
	928	100,610	2,196	70,227	3,124	170,837
Average of 6	155	16,768	— 366	11,704	— 520	28,473

From this accurate abstract of most authentic records [*], we see the full extent of the colonial ship-building which was rapidly encreasing at the æra of revolt. If all the vessels, which were yearly register-ed and sent to sea, from the colonies, had been annually introduced into the foreign trade of Britain, they could have only amounted to *five hundred and twenty*. If the shipwrights of the colonies had supplied

our

[*] With a truly sceptical temper, which often proceeds from ignorance more than from captiousness, some men object even to those authentic records, which were kept by the American Register of Shipping, as not containing the exact number of ships that were built in the colonies. A few remarks will shew with what propriety this objection is made to the authenticity of that record. 1stly. No vessel that had been built in the plantations could possibly sail from them without a register, which was, in fact, its passport.——— 2dly. This passport could not be obtained for a new built ship, till the builder, or other owners, made oath before the Collector of the Port, as to the place where it had been built with other circumstances; till the same ceremony was performed before the Governors.—— 3dly. When these essential proceedings were concluded the collector entered the ship in his book; whereof he gave a *certificate* to the owners, which, when signed by the Governor, constituted what was called among seamen *The Ship's Register*.—— 4thly. The Collector was bound to transmit to the office of the Register General, a duplicate of all those certificates, which he regularly enter-ed in his books.——5thly. It was from these books, that the abstract in the text was carefully taken, and which must consequently contain the exact number of vessels, that had been registered in the plantations, during the specified years, though not the precise quantity of tons, which the owners had an interest to conceal, yet may be easily inferred, by making a reasonable addition to the given sum.

our traders, which is moſt likely, with their top-
ſail veſſels alone, the annual augmentation of American had only amounted to one hundred and
fifty-five. To thoſe who delight, in tracing the
minute variations of commerce, it will afford no
ſmall gratification to be told, that the American
citizens have lately purchaſed ſeveral Britiſh built
veſſels in the Thames; in order to enable them to
carry on the trade between the United States and
the Britiſh Weſt-Indies. And thus, if we wiſely
adhere to our laws, ſhall we, in our turn, ſupply
the Americans with ſhips.

When the ſtatement of our ſhipping was exhibited by the Weſt India Committee, as it appeared in Lloyd's regiſter, immediately before the
war; when ſomething like a demonſtration was
given of our inability to fill up the places of *two
thouſand American ſhips*; all theſe ſtruck well meaning minds as a Gothic ruin, which inſpires melancholy ſentiments and at the ſame time forces the
unwelcome recollection, that all things muſt fall.
But, that frightful fabrick has been now more
nearly examined, and it is at length found to be
one of thoſe magnificent and maſſy ſtructures,
which noblemen, whoſe opulence is equal to their
pride of family, ſometimes erect on the Gothic
plan; and which either gratifies the beholder
by its novelty, or exhilerates by the appearance
of uncommon wealth and great ſkill combined
together.

P 2   Having

Having thus been affured, " *That the American fhipping employed in the foreign trade of Britain amounted to a good deal more than half the Britifh,*" we fhall find fome advantage, perhaps a little amufement, in running up fuccinctly to the original caufe of thofe memorable effects. The year 1638 is the epoch of the arrival of the firft New-England built fhip in the Thames; as we may know from the books of Privy Council. Amid the diftractions of the fubfequent civil wars the New-Englanders became the carriers of the Weft-India products to England ; as appears by the news-papers of thofe times, which are preferved in the Mufeum. The Act of Navigation confirmed their right to do fo, by declaring American built fhips to be completely Englifh. Sir Jofiah Child foon after that declaration warned the nation of the profpective danger of allowing colonies to build fhips for their mother country. Dr. D'Avenant remonftrated in 1698 : " If we fhould go to cultivate among the American plantations the art of navigation and teach them to have a naval force, they may fet up for themfelves and make the greateft part of our Weft-India trade precarious ; befides many other evils, in encouraging them to do fo, it would carry from hence a great number of artificers, which in cafe of a war would be wanting in England." Of that prophecy we have lived alas ! to fee the fulfilment. But, writers wrote then, as writers write now, without much effect on public councils.

During

During the wars of Anne the Parliament encouraged the Colonists to execute those very nautical projects, which those two able statesmen had shewn to be abfurdly dangerous. The shipwrights of the River came up to Whitehall, in 1725, with a complaint, that their busines declined and their workmen emigrated, because the plantations furnished England with ships. Their petition was referred to the lawyers: But, the lawyers answered, they might as well complain of shipbuilding at Bristol; for the American built ships were English. The answer of the lawyers was sent to the Board of Trade for their advice: And they advised, " To lay a duty of five shillings a ton on all American built vessels, which should be employed in the *foreign* trade of Britain." The Ministers did nothing in the end. And the shipwrights remained quiet, though they found their complaints to be unavailing, because faction did not mingle in their grievances. Those who look below the surface of public affairs, as they run down the current of time, will not be surprized, when they are told: That neither the lawyers, the Board of Trade, the Ministers, nor the carpenters, knew the true ground of the grievance, which consisted in this: The plantation built ships were admitted into the ports of Britain with all the exemptions of British; but, the British built ships, when they arrived in the Colonies, were liable to tonnage duties and to other taxes from which their own vessels were altogether exempted. And thus the Colony carpenters enjoyed a double monopoly against

the

the Britifh fhipwrights. The Colony carpenters entered into free competition with the Britifh fhipwrights in all the dominions of the Crown and even beyond them; while the Britifh fhip-wrights could enter into no competition with the Colony Carpenters, in their own ports. And we have feen the melancholy effects, which had flowed from the fountain of thofe caufes, before the epoch of the civil war.

The independence of the United States has hap-pily freed the empire from *the evil*, for which the Minifters of George the Firft could find no remedy, however much it diftreffed one of the moft im-portant of our induftrious claffes. Yet, is it pro-pofed to introduce this embarraffing evil anew. And it is preffed on the public upon pretexts as un-true in fact, as they are unphilofophical in prin-ciple : That we have not capital enough ; that we have not fufficient materials ; that to exhauft the timber of the kingdom which is proper for large fhips would at leaft be impolitic ; and that to build veffels with imported timber will never anfwer. But, it is admitted, that the demand for a new ftock of fhips will be gradual, as the American fhips and the late tranfports wear out.

It is an incontrovertible anfwer to all thofe ob-jections, that the inconvenience is gradually to ap-proach, which will furnifh opportunities enow to provide fufficient relief. We fhall want capital indeed, if we allow the merchants of London and Briftol, of Liverpool and Glafgow, to do now what they formerly did, to fend agents and money to

our

our remaining colonies, or to the United States, to build ſhips for our foreign trade. The laws, as they now operate, (provided no alteration is made) will force our traders to employ that capital, which formerly enriched the induſtrious claſſes in the now United States, to give employment and food to the *real* Britiſh ſubjects, who reſide on the Creeks of Wales and Rivers of Scotland. At the obſcure ports of Wales (a country which abounds with excellent timber for ſhipbuilding) many ſhips have been built, during the war, as we may learn from Lloyd's Regiſter itſelf. And ſince the peace, ſhip timber has been found in commodious parts of Scotland, where trees were ſuppoſed never to have grown. By thus excluding American competitors we ſhall augment the race of ſhipwrights and the public as well as private intereſts will be promoted, by introducing gradually from Scotland and Wales, competitors even into the Thames, by means of their cheaper fabricks. It was owing to a ſimilar competition among the Dutch; who by appropriating the foreſts of woodier countries, build ſuch a multitude of ſhips; and who are thereby enabled to carry the products of the earth at lower freights than any people in Europe. The foregoing conſiderations, with regard to this intereſting part of our domeſtic œconomy, will induce (as we may reaſonably hope) the wiſe government of the iſland of ſhips to remove the taxes, which are payable on the import of naval ſtores of every kind, ſince they

ought

ought to be furely deemed the *raw materials* of the
moft important of *our manufactures* *.

But

* It may be agreeable to men of bufinefs, as well as to men
of fpeculation, to be informed of the *prefent rates* of fhip-
building, in the Southern harbours of England ; as they
were communicated by an intelligent perfon, who made a
tour with a view to difcover the fhip-yard, the cheapeft and
beft.

In the RIVER and BRITISH CHANNEL :
At Gravefend, Broad Stairs, Dover, and
  Folkftone,   ——   ——   £.8 0 0 per ton.
At Hurftake, Cowes, Southampton,
  Weymouth, Tingmouth, Bridport,
  Topfham, Shotham, Dartmouth and
  Cawfand,   ——   £.7 0 0 to 7 10 0
    In the BRISTOL CHANNNEL. (Englifh fide.)
At Biddeford and Barnftable,   —— 6 10 0
    In the BRISTOL CHANNEL, (Wales)
At Newenham, Gatecomb, Chepftow,
  Newport, Hyth, and Swanfey, 6 10 0 to 7 10 0
For thofe prices the workmen engage to compleat the hull
with joiner's work, carved work, and the work of painters,
glaziers, &c. without any extra charge. All thofe fhip-yards
(and indeed all the fhip yards of the kingdom) have been
full of employment, fince the peace. It is this fulnefs which
erects many other fhip-yards. And it is the eftablifhment of
new fhip-yards, which, by means of competition, reduces the
price of manufacture to the loweft poffible point. We are
told, " That the fhip-builders of New-England will contract to build fhips at £.3 fterl. per ton, including the joiner's
work." If an American built fhip will laft *feven* years and a
Britifh built fhip *twenty-one* ; why then the Britifh fhip-
building will prove cheapeft at laft. On fuch occafions it is
not worth while to difpute about *farthings*. Even after the
American built fhips had arrived in the Thames they ufed
to require expenfive additional joiners work, &c. on the
hull.

But, let us return to the propofed meafure of fupplying the Britifh Weft Indies with lumber, whence we have wandered wide, in anfwer to objections of no little weight· For, it had been vain to propofe the furnifhing of our Weft Indies with lumber from our own ports, if we have not a fufficiency of fhipping. The requifite lumber may be divided into two kinds; that which is demanded by the builder; and that which is required by the cooper; and it is intended to difcufs briefly each of them in its order. It is underftood that the larger pieces, which are required for the conftruction of mills and for fimilar purpofes, are found on the plantations, where timber, clofe of grain and difficult of manufacture, grows in great abundance: It is confequently the lighter fcantlings and boards, which planters import from afar. And they may find men enow in London, who will contract to fupply them from the Baltic on the following terms:

One

One ton, or 40 cubic feet, of fir timber,
    will be delivered in the Thames,
    during peace, at   —   £.1 8 10

The fawing of one ton, by hand, fuppof-
    ing four cuts to be made, which will
    produce nine fcantlings, will coft   0 4 0

The freight of one ton to the Weft
    Indies, confidering how many ladings
    are wanted, may be deemed high at   0 18 0
                           ————
                        £.2 10 10

Charge of loading and unloading — 0 2 6
                        £.2 13 4

But, deduct the duty on import, on the
    fuppofition that it is drawn back   0 3 4
                        ————

The coft of delivering one ton in the
    Weft Indies   —   —   £.2 10 0

Deals of 12 feet long 1½ inch thick,
    and 120 in number will be equally
    delivered in the Thames, at   £.7 10 0

Charge of loading and unloading   0 3 0

Freight of 120 to the Weft Indies — 2 0 0
                        ————
                        £.9 13 0

But, deduct the Cuftom-houfe duty,
    which is the fame on 120 deals of
    3 inches thick, and 20 feet long   1 13 0
                        ————

Coft of 120 deals in the Weft-Indies   8 0 0

Something

Something doubtlefs would be faved were the
fhips permitted to fail directly from the place of
loading to the Weft-Indies : But, the giving of
that indulgence would open a very large door. If
a regard to our domeftic quiet would permit us
to erect faw mills ; to be worked either by wind, or
water, or fteam, the Weft-Indians might be fupplied
ftill cheaper : And were we in fuperaddition to that,
great facility to allow all duties on import to be
regularly drawn back, which is altogether confiftent with our modern policy, we might furnifh the
markets of Spain and Portugal with thofe bulky
articles, which are fent them at prefent by the
Dutch, who fetch them from Norway and the
Baltic. During the reign of Anne we firft gave
bounties to our Colonifts, for fupplying us with
naval ftores and wood, that we might not be dependent on Denmark and Sweden : The time is
now come, when the Americans may force us by
their ingratitude to give bounties to Denmark and
Sweden, that we may be independent of the United
States. Such are the revolutions of the world :
It is the bufinefs of wife men to make the moft of
them as the world rolls on : Such is the confequence of conftantly running into extremes : We
favoured and encouraged our colony commerce ;
we debilitated other branches of traffic, by with-
drawing capital and invefting it in our Plantation
trade ; till the extent of our colony commerce
became a deplorable evil. We all remember how
much our manufacturers ufed to be frightened by

Q 2   the

the non-importation agreements of late times: We are again bullied by threats of the loss of a great and neceſſary market for our manufactures. Let us ſhew the United States, by the firmneſs of our conduct, that we can ſupply the Weſt-Indies independent of them; that we ſhall conſider every tax laid by the American Aſſemblies on the importation of Britiſh manufactures, as a deſirable meaſure, for leſſening the evil, of which we complained, and the encreaſe of which we may find cauſe to lament.

We ought to learn from the New Englanders and even from the French how to form thoſe miſcellaneous cargoes, which are ſo commodious to the Weſt-India buyer as well as to the Britiſh ſeller. We might ballaſt our Weſt-India ſhips with ſlate and tiles for the coverings of houſes. The lower hold might be filled with beef and other ſalted proviſions. The flour, meal, peaſe, beans, oats, ought all to be packed in puncheons ready prepared for the filling of rum: The tightneſs of ſuch packages would long preſerve thoſe periſhable articles in a ſultry climate, by excluding the cauſes of corruption. Rum puncheons, that ſhould be ſent as packages, without the payment of freight, might be afforded at 25s. each; which is as cheap as could reaſonably be wiſhed for. A thouſand other articles might in the ſame frugal manner be ſent to the Weſt-Indies for ſupplying their wants. They furniſh themſelves timber, which is eaſily converted

verted into hogſheads for ſugar: Where this re-
ſource failed they might make very good packages
for ſugar from deals of Norway. Let no man
deride this Dutch œconomy. It is ſurely the duty
of the Legiſlature to check magnificent projects of
commerce and unfrugal opperations in ſhipping;
where that ſalutary meaſure may be eaſily executed, by remaining inactive and ſilent, notwithſtanding the efforts of viſionary theoriſts, or the
clamours of intereſted coloniſts. And it ought to
be conſtantly remembered, that the frugality of the
French, from the peer to the peaſant, will ultimately degrade the greatneſs of Britain; if the
moſt rigid œconomy is not obſerved in our modes
of life, the working of our manufactures, the
tranſactions of our commerce, the regulation of
our Colonies, as well as in the adminiſtration of
our Government.

While a ſpirit of moderation prevails in a
trading nation, ſays the profound Sir James Steuart,
it may reſt aſſured than in as far as it excells the
communities with whom it correſponds in this
particular, ſo far will it increaſe the proportion of
its wealth, power and ſuperiority over them. To
gain theſe great objects in modern times, a prudent
legiſlator muſt inſpire his people with a ſpirit
of emulation, in the exerciſe of temperance,
œconomy and an application to labour and ingenuity. It was with a view to theſe ſalutary objects, that it was anxiouſly urged to extend the
manufacture of ſhip building in Britain; that it was
                                                    lately

lately propofed to enlarge the bufinefs of coopers, by furnifhing the Weft-Indies with ready made cafks. For, it was recollected, that the fitting of our fleets had been retarded, by the combination of carpenters, at the commencement of the late war; that both public and private bodies had been obftructed, by fimilar agreements among the coopers; at a time too when the journeymen coopers on the Thames were receiving for their labour fifteen fhillings a day, without having raiment for themfelves or fhelter for their wives. When a body of troops were fent from the Clyde, in 1776, Scotland could not furnifh coopers enow to anfwer the fpeedy demand for packages, though ftaves abounded: And the intelligent and active men, who were intrufted with the victualling of that body of troops, collected coopers from the moft diftant parts of England. An armament then may be delayed or even defeated, amid the preffures of war, by the paucity, or the combination of coopers, which may be produced equally by the incitement of our factions, or by the money of our foes. But, combinations can only be prevented by augmenting the numbers of the defective claffes: The augmentation of numbers can alone be gained by additional employments: And thus combinations among tradefmen may be prevented, or beat down, by raifing up many competitors among the extravagant workmen, whofe fervices are wanted the moft, both in peace and war. It is furely wifer to guard by forefight againft public

difap-

difappointments, than to folace our misfortunes by the downfall of a Minifter, who may have been merely unable, from the paucity or combination, of coopers, carpenters and failors, to execute a meafure without the reach of poffibility.

But in oppofition to the propofed meafure of fupplying the Weft Indians with lumber from the ports of Britain, which has been fhewn to be a recurrence only to the firft principle of colonization, we fhall be confidently told: " That then the fugar would not be worth to the grower the expence of raifing it." Let us firft admit the fact to be true ; and fecondly enquire, what would be the difadvantage to Great Britain. Is it the intereft of Britain that Britifh fubjects fhould poffefs eftates, of the boafted value of fifty millions, which, while fituated in another hemifphere, are more profitable to the owners than eftates within the kingdom ? Is it the intereft of any country, that the attention of its people fhould be conftantly fixed upon a richer world ? From fad experience Spain will anfwer; it is not. Or, is it the peculiar intereft of Britain, confidering her prefent circumftances, to turn the whole energy of her opulent and induftrious claffes upon herfelf, with a view to domeftic employments and national meliorations. It furely is. But, it is further urged, that by having beyond an extenfive ocean, fettlements which muft occupy our people in the fupplying them, and which require many fhips to bring their products away, the tranfatlantic plantations become

thus

thus more advantageous to the State, than if they
were placed in the circumjacent feas. Be it fo.
Yet, if the fupply and the freights are relinquifhed by Britain, what will remain as compenfa-
tions for the irreparable diminution of her induftrious people and the vaft expence of defending diftant dominions, which are impotent in themfelves and yield no revenue or refource ?

If an accidental fcarcity fhould induce the Weft
Indians to appply to the neutral iflands, in their
neighbourhood, for what they may want ; if avarice fhould induce them to continue a practice,
which accident began ; Great Britain would be
thereby driven to the dilemma of either depriving
the Weft Indies of veffels proper for fuch a traffic ;
or of declaring them independent. If the Weft
Indians expect protection from Great Britain,
they muft ftudy to be ufeful to her.

3. But, while the ufefulnefs of the Britifh Weft-
Indies continues, they thereby merit (and thereby
alone merit) every aid and every facility which
Great-Britain can give, confiftent with her naval
policy and domeftic inerefts. The United States furnifhed formerly an extenfive market for the peculiar products of the Britifh Weft Indies, as thofe
offered conftant markets for much of the productions of the United States ; who without the Weft
Indies would not eafily find places of fale for all
the furplufes of an extenfive agriculture. Thus
were they mutually advantageous to each other,
though it may be eafily proved, that the balance of
benefits

benefits ſtood on the ſide of the revolted Colonies: And thus may we ſee, that it would be
inconvenient to both to loſe the gainful cuſtom of
each other; though the greateſt gain may be
be bought at too high a price. Rum was the article of chief demand of the one and ſupply of the
other: And rum is the bewitching commodity, for
which, if the United States, by changing the nature
of their palates, ſhould refuſe to conſume, it would
be very difficult to find an adequate market. This
unfortunate truth we may learn from the following
Cuſtom-houſe entries: There were imported into
the now United States from the Weſt Indies;

In 1770 — 3,250,060 gallons
71 — 2,180,060
72 — 3,332,750
73 — 3,049,298
Annual average ——————— 2,953,042.

This was doubtleſs a large quantity; which
however was not all conſumed in the country;
ſince much was again exported, by means of a circuitous commerce. We may gueſs, rather than infer, the real extent of the conſumption, by deducting
the amount of the quantity ſent out, from the number of gallons, which we have ſeen already brought
in from the Britiſh Weſt Indies. By attending to
the following detail we ſhall diſcover the genuine
meaſure of each particular country's ſupplies from
the American ports.

R   Rum

RUM EXPORTED from the UNITED STATES:

To	1770 West Ind. Gallons.	1770 New Eng. Gallons.	1771. West Ind. Gallons.	1771. New Eng. Gallons.	1772 West Ind. Gallons.	1772 New Eng. Gallons.	1773 West Ind. Gallons.	1773 New Eng. Gallons.
To Britain —— ——	36,632	600	4,015	3,602	4,674	117	10,963	961
Ireland —— ——	10,704	7,931	4,875	4,560	20,259	1,815	23,250	1,240
South of Europe, &c.	9,251	45,310	2,140	38,962	640	37,914	6,688	68,412
Africa —— ——		292,966	120	234,317	9,832	371,334	530	419,366
West Indies, Spanish Main, &c. ——	1,020	2,574	860	5,151	1,915	6,115	2,078	12,057
Nova Scotia, Canada and Newfoundland,	52,712	590,748	36,873	550,514	47,736	520,525	50,716	698,025
	110,319	910,129	48,883	837,106	85,056	937,820	94,225	1,110,061

Average of annual export } 1,041,149.

Such is the view which the Cuftom-houfe entries exhibit of the vaft commerce of Rum; yet,
were there doubtlefs confiderable quantities, both
imported, and fent out, of which there were no
regular reports. The provincial duty in Canada gave rife there, as taxes have done in more
vigilant governments, to the frauds of fmuggling,
to no fmall extent. It is known, that the New-
Englanders fupplied the fifhers of Newfoundland
with many hogfheads of that exhilerating fpirit,
which were not entered at the Cuftom-houfe. It
is equally certain, that the New-Englanders ufed
to fmuggle the rum of their own diftilleries, in
abundance, together with fmall quantities of Weft-
India, into the Orkney and Shetland iflands, and
upon the fhores of Wales. It is furely no inconfiderable advantage, which the wifdom of our councils may draw from the independence of the United
States, that the Britifh Weft Indies will now enjoy
the fole fupply of fo great a demand, as the confumption of Nova Scotia, Canada and Newfoundland; which with the augmentation of the people
and their power to confume muft grow daily
greater: And, in fact, the fupplies of the United
States were no fooner ftopped than rum was fent
in exuberance to all thofe fettlements from the Weft
Indies and even from Britain. The Weft Indies,
or perhaps the Britifh diftilleries, will now profit
from furnifhing our African factories with no inconfiderable quantity of a liquor, which the Afri-

cans,

cans, with the rage of every uncivilized people, prize beyond gold itfelf.

But a market for many gallons muſt neverthelefs be found, if the anger of the United States ſhould prove too powerful for their defires of gratification. The confumption of Weſt-India products by the Iriſh has rapidly encreafed with the accumulations of their number and wealth : And this truth we may infer from the fubjoined detail *.

The annual confumption, according to a feven years average, ending

		Rum Gal.		The Sugar Cwt.
with	1763, was	543,717	—	0
	1770	1,558,097	—	158,846
	1777	1,729,652	—	196,500

We may thence reafonably prefume, that Ireland, having now gained a free trade with the world and a direct trade to the Weſt-Indies, muſt confume greater quantities of both thofe articles, in proportion as ſhe happily enjoys greater bleſſings. Among the numerous improvements, in finance and in commerce, which Britain is preparing to make, under the influence of a mind of great extent and energy, we may prefume, that the traffic of rum will be extended, either by lowering the duties, by changing the mode of collection, or above all, by fuppreſſing the frauds of the fmuggler. Every grievance of which the Weſt-Indies have lately complained has arifen not from actual ſuf-

fering,

* From the Appendix of Mr. A. Young's Tour in Ireland.

fering, but from mere fpeculation. The demand
for all their produdls has been great, fince the
peace, and the price has continued high in proportion. The Weft-Indians have not much to
fear from the threats of the United States: For,
though their Congrefs may poffibly refolve, yet
their citizens will continue even afterwards to
fmuggle, as they formerly did : They fmuggled
Britifh manufadlures, from Holland and New-
York, during a rancorous war : They now fmuggle
their flour into the Havannah, in the face of im-
prifonment and death. For the fugar, molaffes,
and other Weft India produdls, it will not be difficult to find adequate markets, by means of the
vaft circle of the Britifh trade with the world.
And thus much with regard to the manner in
which the Weft-Indies have been hitherto affedled,
or are likely to be affedled, by the recent regulations of the Privy Council.

Sudden changes in the political œconomy of
fuch a nation as Britain, whofe affairs become
daily more complex, from the clafh of different interefts, ought to be regarded with anxiety and
prevented with care. With what dread was the
threatened annihilation of our American trade by
the Congrefs, in 1774, viewed by the boldeft of
our Statefmen, who thought they faw the whole ma-
nufadturers of England already arrived at Whitehall.
Yet, never did an event, which threatened fuch
devaftations in its courfe, pafs away with fo little
mifchief and fo much filence, becaufe its effedls
were unfelt. And in proportion as it added to

our

our ſtock of experience, it conferred many benefits
on the nation, which that memorable meaſure was,
intended to ruin.   Though we have thus acquired
an indubitable privilege to be confident we can
have no right to relinquiſh our prudence and our
caution.   It is impoſſible to foreſee all the commercial difficulties, which may ſtill ariſe, though
none have been hitherto felt, from the independence of the United States.   And it is ſurely wiſe,
though we have learned to think little of American
threats, to enquire what conſequences, either good
or evil, would reſult to the general commerce and
navigation of Britain, from the admiſſion of American ſhips into the Britiſh Weſt-Indies.

Great-Britain from a regard to her ſafety has
long excluded the ſhips of aliens from carrying on
her trade from port to port, on her ſhores, and
from Britain to Guernſey and the other circumjacent iſlands.   The coaſt-trade, next to our internal traffic, merits the greateſt encouragement,
becauſe the ſailors employed in it are moſt *within
call,* by returning moſt frequently into domeſtic harbours.   And owing to the excluſion of foreigners,
the ſhips, which were employed before the revolt
in the *coaſt trade,* were to the ſhips engaged in the
foreign commerce of England, as 220,000 tons are
to 335,000, excluſive of repeated voyages.   If the
ſhores of the Britiſh Weſt-Indies may be regarded
as the coaſts of the empire, though not of the
realm, their navigation ought to be conſidered as
within the meaning, if not within the letter of the
law.

law. And the admiffion of the American veffels, either great or fmall, into the Weft-India ports would amount, in effect, to the impolicy of allowing the Dutch to carry coals from Newcaftle to London.

The regulation of the Statute of Charles II *. whereby alien fhips were excluded from the trade of our coafts, arofe from three effential principles; 1ftly. It preferved the profit of freights to the nation individually; 2dly. By forming a nurfery of feamen it contributed to the fafety of the people collectively;—3dly. By preventing aliens from knowing accurately our harbours and our bays with the fhoals and the rocks, which obftruct the approach of an unfkilful enemy, that circumftance alone contributes to augment the thoufand advantages, which refult in war, from the ignorance of the foe. Of all thefe in their order, as they apply to the admiffion of the American veffels into the Britifh Weft-Indies.

1ft. The profit of freights is of greater importance to Britain than the mines of Potofi are to Spain, becaufe the one ftrengthens, while the others enfeeble the unhappy nation to which they belong. Whence may we infer of how much advantage it is to preferve and extend the navigation of the Weft-Indies, which, from the bulkinefs of their products and their fupplies, employ many fhips.

* 12 Cha. II. Chap. 18. Sec. 6. But, this falutary regulation was firft eftablifhed in the wifer reign of Elizabeth, by 5 Eliz. Chap. 5. Sec. 8.

ſhips. There were engaged in the traffic between
the United States and the Britiſh Weſt-Indies, immediately preceding the revolt, no fewer than
1610 veſſels (including repeated entries) which
bore 115,634 tons; which were navigated by
9718 men; and which tranſported the vaſt American cargo of the value of half a million: And
this intercourſe the Weſt-India Committee aſſure
us, " was carried on almoſt wholly in American
bottoms."

Ingenious men have calculated the value of thoſe
freights in various ways: Say they, lumber, being
of little worth, in proportion to its bulk, and oc-
cupying two thirds of the tonnage outwards, was
carried at the high rate of a hundred *per cent.* on
the original coſt, while the freight of proviſions,
cumberſome as they are, amounted to nearly as
much. To theſe data the Committee have added
their teſtimony, by remarking, " that the American veſſels brought their bulky commodities to
our conſumption at perhaps the cheapeſt rate poſſible, but ſtill *the expence of its tranſportation exceeded
its original value.*" But, it is propoſed, as a mode of
calculation, more accurate and ſpecific, to allow
45 *per cent.* on the value of the outward cargo of
£. 500,000, including the accuſtomed charges of
wages, intereſt, tear, and wear, and proviſions,
and then the freight would amount to £. 225,000;
to charge five *per cent.* on the value of the in-
ward cargo to the United States, amounting to
£. 400,000, and the freight inwards would be
£. 20,000:

£ 20,000 : And the refult of both muft neceffarily be £.245,000. The fame ingenious men more-over infift from actual trial, that were the freights calculated upon the tonnage in the accuftomed mode, the deduction would be nearly the fame. If the value of thofe freights fhould amount to nearly that annual fum, it cannot furely admit of a queftion, whether fo large an yearly profit ought to be relinquifhed to aliens, or preferved to fub-jects : In the one cafe it would augment the wealth of rivals : in the other it would fwell the ftocks of friends.

If contrary to our genuine interefts we fhould allow the American citizens the freights amounting thus to £.245,000 a year, they would carry off that confiderable fum in bullion, fince the balance on the general payments is much in their favour : If, on the contrary, the freights fhould be paid to Britifh fhip-owners they would naturally inveft the amount in trade, by purchafing the products of the country. Were the American veffels admitted. the American citizens would not only carry off the freights in bullion, but, they would gain the profit on the cargo : By excluding our rivals, Britifh fub-jects, who fuftain the Britifh Government, will natu-rally gain both, with the factorage and other profits. If the good fenfe of the nation fhould decide, (and it generally decides right at laft) that Britifh veffels fhall alone carry on that extenfive trade, it muft con-fequently follow, that a proportional quantity of fhipping muft always be found. Of the amount

S   that

that supply we may determine from the subjoined "Account of the number of vessels, their tonnage and men, which were employed in trading between the revolted Colonies and the British West Indies, according to a three years average ending with 1773, and rating each vessel but once every year:

	Ships.	Tons.	Men.
	533	38,544	3339
To which may be properly added one half for other American-owned vessels, which were employed in the Honduras and other branches of West-India trade —	266	19,272	1669
	799	57,816	5008

It has been shewn, that Britain can furnish, this number of vessels, great as it is; that Britain ought in good policy to build them. Of the sagacious œconomy of Holland, which imports the materials of ship building, it is said that were the innumerable busses, which are annually employed in fishing, to return without any success, the community would be greatly benefitted, by the gains that had accrued to the numerous classes, who had been concerned in the original outfit. And the landowners of Britain would derive no less advantage from

from the fale of their timber than from the confumption of the various workmen, who muft be
neceffarily engaged in the fitting of fhips : While
the land owners are thus benefitted, by furnifhing
materials and food, the manufacturers of cloth will
derive as great an advantage from the fupplying of
raimant. It was owing to thefe confiderations,
that Sir Jofiah Child remarked upwards of a century ago: Where much fhipping is employed,
whatever becomes of the merchant, who drives the
trade, multitudes of people will be certain gainers;
as his Majefty and his officers of cuftom, befides,
fhipwrights, butchers, brewers, bakers, rope-
makers, porters, feamen, manufacturers, carmen,
lightermen, and all other artificers, who depend
on trade and fhipping; *which indeed, more or lefs,
the whole kingdom doth."*

Of the feven hundred fhips, (to write in round
numbers) which were requifite to tranfport the
Weft India products to Britain, we have feen one
half of them failing thither without a freight. It
is now apparent that the late regulations have given
thofe fhips two chances for freights, where they had
not formerly one : 1ftly, The exclufion of the American fhips will furnifh them with direct loadings of
lumber and provifions for the Britifh Weft-Indies;
2dly, The owners may choofe to carry a cargo of
dry goods as the finer manufactures are called, for
the ports of the United States; and to tranfport
thence a loading of lumber and provifions: This
operation would form a circuitous voyage, which

of

of all others are the moſt profitable, becauſe ſomething is gained by every loading. It is apparent
how much the export of our manufaƈtures would
be thus promoted, by carrying them at the ſmalleſt
poſſible freight: Britiſh veſſels have aƈtually entered into competition with the American, ſince the
peace, in this buſineſs, and even carried away the
cargoes from them, by under-bidding them on
'Change. 3dly, If the Congreſs ſhould prohibit,
or obſtruƈt, this circuitous tranſportation, Britiſh
ſhips would notwithſtanding have one option more,
by excluding the American ſhips from the Weſt-
India ports: They might call at Corke for ſalted
proviſions; they might touch on the Barbary
coaſt for mules and ſheep; they might viſit the
Cape de Verd's for corn and cattle: And they
might in ſuperaddition carry a cargo to Gibraltar,
or the Streights, to Portugal, or the Canaries. All
this is poſſible; and all this by proper manage-
ment might be made extremely gainful, were the
minuteneſs of our diligence equal to the great extent of our capitals. In this manner is the community benefitted by the profit of freights, with the
attendant faƈtorage; which, by adding gradually
accumulation to accumulation, imperceptibly ſwells
the commercial ſtocks of the kingdom.

But, to thoſe ſalutary meaſures it has been ſtoutly
objeƈted by the Weſt-India Committee, that the
veſſels uſually employed in that traffic are too large
and come too ſeldom; ſo that their operations
would produce either an overſtock, by the quantity
which

which they ufually bring, or a famine, by the delay
of their arrival: And to avoid thefe difficulties,
great in appearance, though none in reality, it is propofed to admit the American veffels of the fmaller
fize, carrying fifty tons and under. But, if the frequent return of little fhips are as effential to the
domeftic fupply of the Britifh Weft-Indies, as
pedlars are to Poland, they ought to look for fubftitutes, if they cannot get the principals. And he
who diligently inquires feldom miffes his genuine
object. The Bermudeans are the Dutch of the
American world, who fetch from the North what
the South may require, and who carry the luxuries
of the South to gratify the palates of the North.
They were engaged in this gainful bufinefs by their
fituation, placed as they happily are in the center,
between the American Continent and the American
Iflands; and they were driven to it by their neceffities, fettled as they are on a barren rock, which diligence alone can fructify. And the Bermudeans
annually employed in the Weft-India trade alone,
at the commencement of the civil war, upwards of
one hundred and thirty quick failing floops, which
carried about four thoufand tons * : And of thefe
admirable veffels they were accuftomed to build
every year from 45 to 50 of the cedars, which
fpring up luxuriantly amid a wafte of rocks. In
thofe veffels the Bermudeans ufed formerly to fend
the Weft-Indies, Britifh and foreign, the following

* Infpector General's books.

ing commodities, wherever they may have found them * :

PROVISIONS.

Of Indian corn	—	3,600 bushels.
Yams	—	16,880 lbs.
Peafe and beans	—	600 bushels.
Rice	—	15,720 barrels.
Onions	—	151,000 ropes.
Poultry	—	741 doz.

LUMBER.

Of oak boards and plank		3,300 feet.
Pine ditto	—	152,653 do.
Clapboards	—	3,170 no.
Hoops	—	2,300 no.
Shingles	—	229,000 no.
Staves	—	28,900 no.

The Bermudeans, fince the peace, have engaged once more in this beneficial bufinefs, with the attention and diligence of traders, who are obliged to follow an œconomical commerce : And the Bermudeans have already gained, in exact proportion to the greatnefs of their efforts. Let not the Weft-Indians, while wallowing in wealth, deride the fervices and aid of thofe little men, who as fubjects, at once quiet and active, merit equal protection.

* Infpector General's books.

1ftly,

2dly. From the foregoing detail it is fufficiently evident what a fruitful nurfery for fhip-wrights, and mariners, and coopers, the enjoyment of many freights will always furnifh the public. And nothing can be added to what Sir Jofiah Child has fo fenfibly faid : " This Kingdom being an ifland, it is our intereft, as well for our prefervation, as our profit, not only to have many feamen, *but to have them, as much as may be within call, in a time of danger.*"

3dly. The free admiffion of the American navigators into the Weft India ports, by giving them accurate knowledge, would bring with it no flight danger to the community, or fmall inconvenience to our commerce. We all remember what advantages it gave the Americans in fupporting their revolt, that they were perfectly acquainted with our European and Weft Indian coafts ; that they fpoke the fame language ; and that their perfons and drefs were nearly a like. To allow them to retain that knowledge, while it is dangerous to us, can never be right. During peace they would inveigle the Britifh Seamen into the American fervice. During war they would furnifh our enemies with pilots for every hoftile invafion. Acquainted with every ifland and with every harbour, and fpeaking the fame dialect ; the American navigators, with the morality of feamen, would one day enter the ports as friendly traders ; the next they would land on the coaft as depredatory plunderers : By the firft operation they would dif-

cover

cover the nakednefs of the land : By the fecond
they would carry away the Negroes from the fields,
and cut the fhips from the Bays. Not content
with plunder by land, the American privateers
would prowl among the fhoals of the Bahamas for
the Weft India traders, who, as they returned
through the neighbouring ftreights, might be difperfed by ftorm, or might be unconvoyed by accident. From fuch a ftate of things the danger to
the Weft Indian planters and inconvenience to the
Britifh fhip owners are manifeft. But it is not
eafy to calculate the premiums, which the infurers
would afk to fave harmlefs the unfortunate trader,
during a war of treachery as well as of force.

Thofe are not all the difadvantages that would
neceffarily refult to the commerce and navigation of
the Britifh empire, by admitting the American navigators into the Weft India ports. The Weft Indians loudly clamoured in 1731," That the Northern
Colonifts carried away confiderable quantities of cafh
to the French Iflands, wherewith they bought rum,
fugar, and molaffes." That this complaint was founded we may fuppofe, from its being always continued.
The French then were fupplied with bullion, which
ought to have been remitted to Britain, in payment
of debts. That cafh was often carried to the continental colonies is a fact, which may be proved,
by the direct evidence of the Infpector General's
books : The truth is confirmed, by the ftate of
the balance of trade between them. The value of
the

the annual cargo, which was ufually fent by the revolted Colonies to the Britifh Weft Indies amounted, according to a three years average ending with
1773 to £.500,000 ; the Weft-India products,
which were carried away in return amounted at
£.400,000; and the freights to £.245,000, befides
their profits. Hence, the balance of trade between them rofe to £.345,000. This is not a
fmall fum to be carried off from the Britifh Dominions; and which had been otherwife tranfmitted
to Britain, perhaps in liquidation of ballances. Were
there £.345,000 yearly imported in bullion, that
fountain would probably be fufficient to feed the
ftream of our circulation; which, like the flow
of our Thames, ought to run ——

    " Gentle, yet not dull ;
Strong without rage, without o'erflowing full."

The vaft concatenation of payments, public as
well as private, depends on the fullnefs and flow of
that circulation. The profperity of our manufactures and trade ; the invigoration of our credit ; neceffarily refult from the punctuality of thofe
payments. The induftrious claffes are all enabled
by manufacture, and traffic, and credit, to accu-
mulate favings, (and their accumulations have long
fupported the pillars of the State) which gradually
augment the commercial capital of the kingdom.
And in this manner is it of the greateft confequence
to the general commerce of the empire to exclude
the American veffels from the Weft India ports.

       T   Of

Of a fubject, thus interefting, becaufe our fafety
and our opulence are both involved in its difcuffion,
let us take another view. To thofe who delight, in
tracing the varieties of human character, or in
marking the minute occurrences of human tranfactions, nothing has ever appeared more ftriking, or
unaccountable, than the difference, in policy and
fuccefs, between the Britifh Weft Indies and the
French. The firft was bred in the lap of luxury ;
the fecond was reared in the fchool of misfortune :
The firft was gratified with a government of freedom and indulgence ; the fecond was ruled by a
fyftem of regulations and rigor. The French planter entered the Weft India world with feeble efforts, becaufe he was depreffed by penury ; he
gradually added to his little ftock by his care ; his
attentive profits, however fmall in the beginning,
added accumulation to accumulation ; a plantation of coffee, which required few hands to tend
it, was at length enlarged into a plantation of fugar :
And in this manner the French Weft Indies rofe
up with a rapidity and vigour, which aftonifhed
the inattentive and ignorant, while the Britifh Weft
Indians, who formed a character the direct reverfe
of the French, were conftantly afking protection
and encouragement. But who can fupport the indolent and carelefs, the proud and the magnificent,
who began the world perhaps with borrowed money,
on ufurious intereft ? The French planters found
capitals in their own refources : The Britifh found
capitals in England. And the Britifh Weft Indians

dians have been at all times greatly indebted to Britain for the money, which fettled and improved their fugar-works, which though withdrawn from productive occupations at home could not be eafily brought back from abroad. Fifty million are now faid to be employed in the Weft India eftates : But, if that vaft fum, or even the half of it, could at this moment be revefted in domeftic employments, how much more would it promote the commercial profperity of Britain. To recover debts in our colonies has been a neceffary meafure, which fometimes attracted our legiflative care, without fuccefs. And to admit the Americans into the Weft India ports is to augment a deplorable evil, by enabling the planters to fend thofe products to the United States, which ought to have been tranfmitted to Britain, in part of payment of the intereft and principal of their Britifh Debts.

Of thofe engaging topics let us take a parting view. The New Englanders have long grown rich, by practifing a pedling trade with the revolted Colonies and with the Weft India Iflands. The mifcellaneous cargoes, wherewith they fupplied the American world, were compofed of the various petty articles, which a difperfed people cannot eafily want, yet cannot readily fetch. If the American navigators are admitted into the Weft India ports the New Englanders will extend this gainful traffic and the other American Traders, invited by their gains, will follow their fuccefsful example. Their free intercourfe at prefent with France, Holland, and Hamburgh,

T 2   not

not in their own fhips alone, will greatly facilitate that traffic. Thus the American citizens will fupply the Weft India planters with the filks of France, with the groceries of Holland, and with the linnens of Germany, in oppofition to the manufactures of Britain. The Britifh woollens are unfuitable to the fultrinefs of the Weft India climate and the Britifh linnens and cottons will be rejected for the cheaper linnens of Germany and the more fhewy fabricks of France. Intereft will in this manner concur with vanity to fupport the fmuggler againft the preventive officer. And in this manner will the manufactures of Britain be depreffed, and the morals of the planters corrupted, while the falutary principle of colonization will be circumvented, if not deftroyed.

Having thus introduced rivals to our domeftic manufactures, the American traders would ere long equally interrupt our Eaft India commerce. They have lately fent a veffel from Philadelphia to China. And having thus made a beginning they will be carried forward in their enterprizing progrefs, by the markets which they will find in the Weft Indies, in oppofition to the more expenfive fupplies of our own Eaft India Company. "To wink at fuch proceedings, faid Doctor D'Avenant, in 1698, has been lately the practice of corrupt governors; and if fpeedy care be not taken, thofe abufes will grow too inveterate, or too big for correction. So that in procefs of time, thofe colonies (if they fall

into

into the practice of trading independently of England) may erect themselves into independent commonwealths, or piratical focieties, which at laft
we fhall not be able to mafter; by which means
the plantations, that are now a main branch of our
wealth, may become a ftrength to be turned againft
us." And in this manner would the commerce
and navigation of Britain be injured, nearly in the
proportion, wherein the American veffels fhould
be admitted to traffic in the Weft India ports.

§. 3. The attentive reader, having thus feen
the channel of our American trade freed from every
obftruction, and fuch falutary regulations eftablifhed, as require few amendments, is at length
impatient to know, what neceffity there is for a
commercial treaty with the United States, or what
advantages it would bring to Great Britain, were it
already agreed on. It is now propofed to anfwer
queftions, which involve our domeftic quiet and
foreign interefts, by a very fhort difcuffion.

The origin of commerce may be traced up to
that moft early epoch the introduction of property
among mankind. When the individual was allowed to appropriate, what fupplied his wants, or
promoted his convenience, he acquired a right,
that could not be divefted, without his confent,
which introduced trade, or by force, which gave
rife to war. In this manner men, from obferving
each others needs and refpecting the poffeffions of
each, learned the arts of mutual commutation, by
finding an equivalent, which by an eafy progrefs
fettled

settled into traffic with all its varieties. Freedom is essential to commerce, because consent is always implied : When compulsion is introduced warfare in the same moment begins. Yet, the liberty of all must. necessarily arise from the restraint, which is imposed on the appetites of each, since it is the clash of many wills, that produces anarchy, the worst foe of freedom. And hence we may infer the truth of the celebrated position of Montesquieu that the constraint of the merchant is *not* the constraint of trade.

The association of many individuals, to regard each others rights, and to redress each others wrongs, formed a community. The various modifications of mens passions, their likes and dislikes, gave rise to many communities. But, as the compacts, which bound the associators together, no further restrained mens previous privileges, than was essential to the being and end of the compact, it necessarily followed, that the community collectively enjoyed the rights of individuals separately. Societies learned ere long, that they too had wants, which could only be satisfied, by sending equivalents to neighbouring tribes. And hence arose the commerce, between neighbouring communities, and by means of navigation, between the most distant ones. In this new communication the same liberty of choice and the same restraint of appetite prevailed, as there had existed in the traffic of individuals. Hence, though every state had a right to communicate its wants and to offer its equivalents, every other body of men possessed feffed the fame privilege of judging with regard to the value of thofe equivalents, by fetting a higher price on its furplus products, which it may even refufe to fell, when the buyer acts unreafonably.

From thofe fimple principles the writers on the law of nations have juftly inferred, that the obligation of trading with a foreign country is a right, neceffarily *imperfect*, fince the one party has the fame privilege to determine for itfelf, whether fuch a commerce would be detrimental, as the other had to offer its equivalents, adopting reafon as the guide, becaufe nothing which is unreafonable can ever be right. But, every fociety being obliged, fays Vattell, to trade with others, only as far as it can without being wanting to itfelf, the fuccefs of the tranfaction will always depend on the judgment each State fhall form of what it can and ought to do in particular cafes: The freedom of trade depending generally on the judgment of another muft be always uncertain, and the right of commerce muft confequently be ever imperfect. In this manner were *commercial treaties* introduced among mankind, in order to fecure a conftant rule and punctual tranfactions, which could no longer be broken or varied; without incurring the blame of infringing a compact, that both parties had voluntary formed. Such is the fource to which jurifts trace up the origin of commercial treaties, which, it is apparent, may in their formations narrow the general right of traffic, and may, in their end, relinquifh more than they had gained.

Every

Every nation having thus a full right to regulate its own commercial affairs, by the rule of what is advantageous, or hurtful, may make those treaties of commerce, which its interest required, and which implies the approbation of another, or it may regulate its foreign, as well as domestic, trade, by its municipal law, which is founded on its own sense of utility, without asking the world's consent. But that regulation is properly said to be alone just and commendable, which is formed with a tenderness for the wants and supplies of mankind, having a regard to the bounds of possibility, and the reasonableness of the measure. And hence it is apparent, that the true mode of judging of every proffered treaty is its salutariness, or dangers, its usefulness, or disadvantage.

Many clamour for a commercial treaty with the United States, without considering for a moment, whether it would be hurtful or convenient ; how far our laws have already established every regulation which our interest requires. Writers have submitted to the world sketches of such projects of traffic, between the two countries, as they thought would be most beneficial and wise, were the Legislature to enact them into rules, that all should be required to obey. It were to be wished, that the same writers had published the draught of a comercial treaty with the United States, that every one might have examined its principles, and approved or condemned its stipulations, as they had stood the test of usefulness, or of disadvantage.

Let

Let us, to fupply this defect fuppofe, that the French Commercial Treaty of 1778, or the Dutch Treaty, which they have not purchafed with their accuftomed caution or œconomy, had been propofed to our acceptance, we fhall thereby have an opportunity of judging of the web, by infpecting the woof and the warp. And with this view it is propofed to examine minutely the treaties, which have been held up as examples to other nations, that we may determine, whether they ought to be accepted, as ufeful, or rejected, as either too trifling, or too unfalutary, or as containing regulations, which our laws have already adopted.

The three Treaties are founded in fimilar principles : The French in perfect equality; the Dutch in reciprocal utility; and the Britifh in liberal equity : And they all three eftablifh peace among the nations, for the continuance of which every wife and good man ought to pray ; fince from war no good can refult; from war with the American States nothing can be gained, but much might be loft. By the French and Dutch Treaties it was mutually agreed : " Not to grant any particular favour, in refpect of commerce and navigation, which fhall not become common to the other." From this ftipulation, which, from the fimplicity of its language, fets all conftruction at defiance, it is apparent enough, That the United States can grant to Great Britain no fpecial immunities, whatever price fhe might be willing to pay : They cannot grant to Great Britain the exclufive privilege of alone fupplying them with her woollens and hardware, in confideration of admitting

U   their

their veſſels into the ports of the Britiſh Weſt-
Indies. Nothing contrary to the tenour of the
treaty can be granted, ſays Vattel, to a third party.
Such excluſive privileges ought not to be accepted,
were it in the power of the United States to confer
them, becauſe monopolies are always viewed with
jealouſy, while they are ſeldom enjoyed to their
full extent. The United States have therefore no
boon to grant, which ought to be regarded as
an equivalent for commercial privileges, that might
be diſadvantageous to Britain. And the two Commonwealths of America and the Netherlands have
avowed, as the baſis of their Commercial Treaty,
" That all burdenſome preferences are the uſual
ſources of debate, embarraſſment and diſcontent."

It is ſtipulated by Article 3, 4, 5, of the French
and Article 2d of the Dutch Treaty,—" That the
people of the Contracting Powers ſhall pay no more,
or greater impoſts, in the ports of each other
than the moſt favoured nations pay, and ſhall enjoy
every exemption in trade and navigation, whether
in ſailing from port to port, in the ſame country,
or in navigating thence to foreign nations." But,
we have already ſeen, that the American citizens,
as merchant ſtrangers, are entitled by our laws *
to the privilege of paying no other duties at our
Cuſtom-houſe, than denizens pay in the moſt
friendly ports : We have ſeen too, what is ſtill
more advantageous, that by our regulations, ſince

the

* From 9 Hen. III. ch. 9; 5 Hen. IV ch. 7; and
12 Char. II. ch. 4. which requires, *that aliens ſhall be honeſtly
entreated as to the payment of taxes*, at the Cuſtom-houſe.

the peace, the United States are freed from the payment of all taxes on the importation of their products; from the payment of those alien duties which all other aliens were then obliged to pay. Whether the Commercial Treaties with France and the Netherlands, or the spontaneous regulations of Britain, convey, in this respect the greatest exemptions and most valuable privileges to the United States, does not therefore admit of a question. France indeed and Holland have allowed the American citizens, as they allow all other aliens, on the payment of superior duties to subjects to participate in their coast trade, which Britain has absolutely denied to them, as she had long denied to every other alien. A regard to her defence and safety established the general rule. And a respect for the law of nations forbids any foreign power from taking umbrage at a domestic measure, so prudent in its origin and so salutary in its consequences.

By the 9th Article of the French Treaty, the ships and mariners of the Contracting Powers were restrained from fishing in any of the havens, creeks, roads, coasts, or places of the others, under the penalty of confiscation; and the United States moreover stipulated not to molest the French in fishing on the Banks or in the vicinity of Newfoundland. On the delicate subject of fishing the Dutch were cautiously silent. On the other hand, by our Treaty of Peace with the United States, they were allowed the full right of fishing on the Banks

U 2   of

of Newfoundland, on the fhores of Nova Scotia and Labradore, with the beneficial freedom of drying their fifh on their unoccupied coafts. The difference then to the United States, between the Britifh and French Treaties, amounts to this, whether the granting, or refufing a favour, is the moft advantageous and kind.

The *droit d'aubane* is relinquifhed by France, and the right of difpofing by teftament is acknowledged by Holland. The Dutch, with their ufual policy have allowed liberty of confcience and of fepulture : But the French are filent on thefe fubjects of religious fcrupulofity. The Dutch thought it of importance to ftipulate ; that parties may employ their own factors or attornies ; that fhip-mafters may be allowed to manage their own affairs and may load and unload with the freedom of fubjects. Were a Britifh ftatefman to boaft of fuch ftipulations he would incite the ridicule of the wits without infuring the approbation of the grave. The law of England, (as we have already feen,) allows every alien friend to difpofe of his effects by teftament, or preferves them for his next of kin. The rights of confcience have been at length recognized ; have been happily adopted into our liberal fyftem. The melancholy privilege of burial our humanity denies neither to the Jew, the Turk, nor the Infidel. And in a country which has been honourably denominated, *The Land of Liberty*, every ftranger may exert his own diligence, or ufe the addrefs of an agent, or engage the abilities of a lawyer.

lawyer. The jurifprudence of the United States fully coincides with the laws of Great Britain, in all thofe refpects. And by all thofe ftipulations the United States gained from France and Holland, who were not exactly informed of American modes, confiderable immunities, without granting equivalents; fince the mere protection of law can with, no propriety be deemed the communication of benefits, which might have been denied.

We may equally apply the foregoing remarks to the various ftipulations of thofe treaties in cafes of fhipwreck; in the protection which is agreed to be given to fhips when purfued by pirates; to the option which is given the owners in the breaking of bulk *. In thofe unfortunate cafes the humanity of the law of England has adopted the memorable declaration of CONSTANTINE: " If any fhip be at any time driven on fhore by tempeft let the owner have it; for what right has my Exchequer in another man's calamity." This fentiment, fo worthy of a great prince, has been adopted and enforced by our own Edward I †. The zeal of our Parliament for the rights of human nature hath declared him a felon, who fhall plunder a ftranded fhip, and him, who with greater malice, fhall exhibit falfe lights on purpofe to bring navigators into danger: And thefe declarations, equally humane as

as

---

* By 28 Ed. III. chap. 13. fec. 3, and 20 R. II. ch. 4, no fhips fhall be conftrained to come into port, or reftrained in felling their goods.

† By 3. Ed. I. ch. 4.

wife, are little more than the revival of the virtuous laws of Henry II, whom no monarch need
be afraid to copy. By the Statute of 31 Henry
VI. ch. 4, which remains ſtill unrepealed, for the
honour of our laws, it was enaćted, " That if any of
the King's ſubjećts attempt, or offend upon the ſea,
or within the King's obeyſance, againſt any ſtranger,
in amity, or under ſafe condućt, eſpecially by attack-
ing his perſon or robbing him of his goods, the Judges
may cauſe full reſtitution and amends to be made to
the party injured." And by a more modern ſtatute *
it is declared to be piracy to correſpond with pirates,
or to board forcibly any merchant veſſel, though
without forcing, or carrying her off, and deſtroying,
or throwing overboard any of her goods. Let no
foreign navigator therefore doubt, whether he is
entitled to full protećtion from pirates, in the ſeas
and ports of Britain. In a country, where the people have made it an article of their Charter to give
ſecurity to *foreign merchants*, no alien *friend* need fear
for the ſafety of his perſon, his property, or his reputation. And he may learn indeed from Mon-
teſquieu, " That in Britain he has no occaſion to
loſe an infinite deal of time at the Cuſtom-houſe ;
where he has no uſe for a particular commiſſioner
either to obviate all the difficulties of the farmers,
or to ſubmit to them." Whether, on this head
of the ſubjećt, the treaties of Holland and
France, or the laws of Great Britain, are the
most

* 8 Geo. I. ch. 24.

moft honourable in their origin, the moft effica-
cious in their operation with regard to the United
States, is a queftion, which requires furely no further illuftration.

But, the more to facilitate the commerce of the
United States, France has ftipulated to grant them
one or more free ports, in Europe, and to continue
to them the free ports, which had been already
opened in the French Weft Indies. If that is a
fiee port, where goods may be freely landed without paying a duty, Great Britain has already eftablifhed various free ports within the Kingdom. In
them the tobaccos of the United States may be
landed without any expence : All their other unmanufactured products, which prudence allowed
them to bring, may be entered without payment of
duties. What France then only ftipulated to do,.
Great Britain has actually done : In the United
States there are higher duties collected on fhipping
and goods of aliens than on thofe of citizens : In
Britain the American citizens pay no taxes on the
importation of their merchandizes : And of confequence Great Britain has done more for the
United States by her laws, than France and Holland have done, by their treaties. When the United
States obtained at length, what they had long
wifhed and lately fought for, the laws of Great
Britain interpofed a bar, between her remaining
Colonies and them. The Britifh Government
opened a Great market in the Britifh Weft Indies
for the products of the United States, by foftening
the

the rigour of those laws, in favour to them, while all other foreigners were notwithstanding shut out. In this view of the subject, the admitting a qualified importation amounted to a qualified free port, which is all that the French have allowed. The design of the act of navigation, says D'Avenant, was to make those Colonies as much dependant as possible upon their mother country. To admit the American ships into the British West Indies, contrary to the policy of that law, is to establish an universal free port and with it the independence of those Colonies. And we have learned from experience, what indeed we might have known without the cost of a hundred millions, that the absolute independence of our transatlantic territories is much more advantageous to Britain than their virtual dependence : In the one case she enjoys all their commercial advantages, without the weighty burthen of their defence : In the other, she is subjected to the vast charge of protecting them, without enjoying any greater benefit from their trade, than all the world enjoys.

We have now fairly compared the commercial advantages, which the United States derive, on the one hand, from their late treaties with Holland and France, and on the other, from the established laws of Great Britain. Let justice decide according to the representations of candour, from which of those sources a wise people might draw the greater benefits, were gratitude placed in the chair of prejudice

There

There are indeed in thofe treaties a variety of
ftipulations relative to a ftate of hoftilities. But,
war is not the bufinefs of life. And every man,
either prudent or humane, ought to wifh, that it
were lefs frequent in its recurrence and lefs extended in its duration. Yet, treaties either to regulate
its commencement, or to direct its operations, are
by no means neceffary. And our laws already
contain every regulation, that a wife people ought
to defire, or a cautious peopleought to grant. " All
merchants, fays OUR GREAT CHARTER, fhall be
fafe and fecure in coming into England, and going
out of England, and ftaying and travelling through
England, as well by land as by water, to buy and
to fell, without any unjuft exactions, according to
ancient and right cuftoms, except in time of war,
and if they be of a country againft us. And if
fuch are found in our dominions, at the beginning
of a war, they fhall be apprehended, without injury of their bodies and goods, until it be known
to us, or to our chief jufticiary, how the merchants
of our country are treated in the country at war
againft us; and if ours are fafe there, the others
fhall be fafe in our country". This is the claufe
which hath juftly conferred celebrity on England.
And of this fignal conftitution Britons may boaft
in every quarter of the globe, where fhips fail, or
merchants-trade. Now, who will fay, that he can
form a treaty, more falutary in its principle, or more
judicious in its means, than the declaration, which
our vigorous anceftors demanded and obtained, at

X   that

that memorable epoch, in favour of merchants and trade.

But, while it is admitted, that the American citizens will derive a thoufand benefits from the emanations of our fyftem, it may be properly afked, what fecurity do Britifh fubjects enjoy from the laws of the United States? Is there reciprocity; is there mutual protection? Yes: It may eafily be fhewn, that the fundamental laws of the United States are exactly analogous to the fundamental laws of Great-Britain, in all thofe rules, which give fecurity to the citizen and protection to the ftranger.

The laws of a people, whatever they may be, are the liberties, to which they are the moft attached, and which they defend with the greateft ardour. The common law, the ancient ftatutes of England, had been all carried by the Englifh fettlers, into the American colonies, as their birth-right, or afterwards adopted by ufage, or fome-times recognized by the pofitive acts of their fubor-dinate legiflatures. It is furely curious to trace the operation of that principle, amidft the un-natural contefts of the parent and her children, about their mutual rights. And we fhall find by' no long refearch, that the revolted colonifts have interwoven the laws of England into the very tex-ture of their fundamental conftitutions, while their animofities were the moft warm and rancorous.

We may learn the truth of that exhilerating pofition, from an examination of what each of the

United

United States thought proper to do, when they
were about to form governments for themselves.—
The conftitutions of New-Hampfhire and Maffachufett's exprefsly provided, " that all laws theretofore ufed fhall remain in force till altered."—
Rhode Ifland and Connecticut retained their ancient forms and laws, which had been at all times
fufficiently democratic and even independent.—
New-York declared, " that fuch parts of the common law and ftatutes of England and acts of
Affembly, as formed the law of the province on
the 9th of April 1775, fhall continue the laws of
the Commonwealth." New-Jerfey followed impli-
citly the example of New-York, as it had always
done. Pennfylvania has made the declaration of
rights part of her fundamental conftitutions. The
Delaware State referved exprefsly the common
and ftatute law as they had been formerly adopted
and practifed. Maryland declared, " that her
citizens were entitled to the common and ftatute
law of England, which had been ufed and approved, in the province. Virginia, with a zeal
which fhewed more of her rancour than her prudence, directed that the executive powers of government fhould be exercifed according to the
laws of the Commonwealth, but fhould under no
pretence exercife any power or prerogative by
virtue of any law, ftatute, or cuftom of England:
Yet, this declaration formed a direction to the
Virginian Governors rather than a fyftem for the
Virginian Judges. And we may prefume that the

general

general web of their jurisprudence had been woven
of the warp of common law and the woof of ancient statutes. We may infer this from their
general revisal * in 1663, when the assembly " endeavoured in all things, as near as the capacity
and constitution of the country would admit to
adhere to those excellent and often refined laws of
England, to which they acknowledged all reverence and obedience." Yet, the principal Virginians were too prudent to leave it in doubt how
far their ancient laws should operate even after the
revolt: And the Assembly passed an act, in 1776;
declaring, " that all the laws formerly in force
should continue, till abrogated." North Carolina
with greater prudence intwined *The Declaration of
Rights* about the root of her fundamental constitution: And with equal wisdom enacted expressly,
in 1777, " that the common and statute law
theretofore used should continue in force." South
Carolina declared, by her original association,
" that all laws then practised should remain till
repealed." Georgia adopted into her fundamental
constitution nothing more than *the Habeus-corpus-
act:* But, if we may believe the affirmation of her
Chief Justice Walton *, " the law of England has
been studded into the Georgian system." And
thus have we found, that the *often refined* laws of
England have been studded into all the American
systems. The American youth still continue to
read

* Laws, p. 1.
* Georgia Gazette, 13 May, 1784.

read Coke upon Lyttelton as their text-book; and
the experienced practiser continues under their new
forms to quote the various reporters of what has
been said and decided in Weftminfter-hall; to
which American Judges ftill pay all the reverence,
which is due to the collected wifdom of that vaft
depofitary of civil wifdom and legal fcience.
And the general jurifprudence of England and
the United States muft confequently be very
nearly the fame, however different the forms of
their government may be.

Having thus eftablifhed the general principle we
may properly enquire, how it applies to Britifh
fubjects, as to the impofing difabilities, or giving
them protection. If the American citizens are
aliens in England, Britifh fubjects muft neceffarily
be aliens within the United States. If any government was ever founded in actual campact the conftitution of the United States muft be allowed to
have originated from the hallowed fource of pofitive ftipulation. But, perfons, who were no
parties to the American affociations, can never be
entitled to the privileges refulting from the American compacts, to members of them. The people
of Europe, who were quiet fpectators of the
ftruggle for independence, are confequently aliens
to the United States. Much more are Britifh
fubjects, who oppofed the formation of thofe con-
federacies, aliens to the American governments.
And in fact we find the European people confidered by the legiflative and judicial powers of
the

the United States altogether as aliens, who are entitled to none of their immunities, fince they owe them no obedience. It was the peace, which converted Britifh fubjeéts, who had been alien *enemies*, into alien *friends*. Now, every privilege and proteétion, which belong to the American citizens, as alien friends, in Britain, equally appertain to Britifh fubjeéts, as alien friends, within the United States, with refpeét to the fecurity of their perfons, their property, and their reputation ; becaufe the laws of both countries are thus fubftantially the fame *. And the jurifprudence of both

countries

---

* It ought not to be concealed, becaufe it militates againft the doétrines maintained in the text, that Walton, the Chief Juftice of Georgia, and his affociates, determined, fince the peace, that Perkins, a Britifh merchant, and alien *friend*, could not fupport an aétion of debt againft a citizen. [Georgia Gazette, 13 May, 1784.] That decifion feems however to have been univerfally reprobated. It may gratify a reafonable defire of information to /fee the opinion of Mr. Stirk, the Attorney-General, and Mr. Stephens, another Georgia lawyer, which was taken the 10th of May, 1784, and publifhed on that fignal occafion, in the fame Gazette :

" The judgment of the Chief Juftice and his affociates, given in Chatham county laft term, (relative to the privilege of Britifh merchants, who remained in Savannah after the evacuation, of fuing the citizens of this State) may be looked upon as laudable, but tranfient charaéters, *although Britifh fubjeéts*, who have arrived fince, claim that right from the duties which they pay to the State, over and above thofe paid by other merchants, who refide here. Should the fountain of juftice be ftopped againft them, and they prohibited from profecuting for their lawful demands, all commerce

will

countries giving thus mutual protection to the inhabitants of both, feems to preclude the neceffity of a commercial treaty, which would be lefs reverenced in its ftipulations, and lefs powerful in its effects.

But, if the eftablifhed laws of the two countries in this manner exclude the neceffity of a commercial treaty we may yet inquire, whether it would be advantageous, or ufeful. "It has been obferved of this nation, faid D'Avenant, in 1698, that we have loft by treaties, what we had gained by valour; that we have been conftantly outwitted

in

will be annihilated, and the greateft diftrefs to the citizens will follow. By the *ftatute* law of England, *which is alfo in full force in this State,* aliens are allowed under that Government to maintain actions for perfonal chattels. Aliens (even Britifh fubjects) in the State of South Carolina are allowed to fue the citizens and are entitled to a jury *medietate linguæ,* in fuits againft them, if they choofe. There have been even tranfient Courts allowed them : And this feems to be founded on the privileges aliens are entitled to in all countries, *except where they are particularly prevented.* Aliens may trade as freely as other people, though fubject to higher duties, and as they are not confidered as citizens in this State pay duties accordingly."

When the Chief Juftice had admitted, by his decifion, *that the laws of England were ftudded into the Georgian fyftem,* he could not, as a logician, or a lawyer, deny the inevitable inference of law : That an alien *friend,* could maintain an action of debt, in the tribunals of Georgia. Little did Mr. Walton reflect, amid the clamours of the times, which ought to have infpired him with caution rather than rafhnefs, *that judgments againft apparent right are confidered by every law as fufficient caufes for granting letters of reprizal.*

in ſtipulations we have made with foreign States
and Princes, as well concerning *intereſt* as *dominion*:
And it is very evident, that they who could never
face us in the field, have over-reached us in the
cabinet; and all along we have ſeemed ſtronger in
a battle, than in council." The unequal agreements of the Portugal treaty, of 1703, had been a
ſufficient juſtification of D'Avenant's remark had
not more modern treaties confirmed it. And it is
owing to the wailings of impatience, the roar of
ignorance, or to the incitements of intereſt, that
our ſtateſmen are conſtantly driven from their
better purpoſe into improvident compacts, and are
often obliged to ſacrifice the real intereſt of their
country to their own quiet. This is a degeneracy
however, againſt which virtuous reſolution ought
always to ſtruggle: And this is a motive for placing
the ſubject of commercial treaties in every poſſible
light; as ſome of them may catch the eye of inat-
tention, or others of them may illuminate the dark
deſigns of avarice, or of faction.

It is ſurely a previous queſtion of no ſmall moment, whether there at preſent exiſts within the
United States, any power, which can lawfully conclude a commercial treaty. By the 9th article of
the American confederations the Congreſs are
inveſted with the *ſole* and *excluſive* right, (nine States
being repreſented in Congreſs) of entering into
treaties and alliances; provided *that no treaty of
commerce ſhall be made, whereby the legiſlative power
of the reſpective States ſhall be reſtrained, from impoſing*
ſuch

such imposts on foreigners, as their own people pay ; or
whereby each State shall be hindred *from prohibiting
the exportation, or importation, of any species of goods
whatever.* These contradictory stipulations created
no new absurdity in the American history and jurisprudence. We all remember the famous resolves
of their colonial representatives in Assembly, during
turbulent times : We the Delegates have the *sole
right* of imposing taxes on the good people of this
Province, *with the consent* of the Upper House, and
Governor. By article the 6th no State without
the consent of the Congress can send any embassy
to, or receive any embassy from, any King, Prince,
or State, or enter into any conference, agreement,
alliance, or treaty with them. Thus, have the
jealousies of the United States prevented the establishment of a competent power, among them, for
the concluding of commercial agreements. And
that fatal conclusion is amply confirmed by recent
experience, which hath shewn us the individual
States busily, perhaps factiously, employed, in
empowering the Congress to regulate commerce,
for the special purpose of retaliation, or redress.

Yet, though armed with all those powers, either
general or particular, the Congress lately sat from
November to June, without executing any measure
of retaliation or redress, on the difficult subject of
their West-India trade. They, on this occasion,
made use of their accustomed intrigues, to incite
the traders to clamour for prohibitions, or at least
restrictions. Meetings of Merchants were held,

in

in different States, in pursuance of instigatory letters, to consider of means to invigorate the Congress, by adding the force of previous assent to the
noise of popular complaint. Yet, fearing perhaps
the renewment of non-importation agreements, or
regarding more their genuine interests, the traders
resolved *in secret*: That Britain, when regulating
her colonial commerce, had done nothing more than
Spain, Portugal, and France, continued to do ;
that though they felt an inconvenience from the
West India restrictions they could not justly complain of an injury ; and that it would be wiser to
consider of modes of circumvention than to adopt
measures of force. In the end the Congress did
nothing, in order to enable individuals to find
means to promote, each his particular interest.

The Congress however, about the beginning of
May 1784, entered into certain resolutions *, by
which

---

* The Continental Journal of Boston, dated the 3d of
June 1784, contains the following resolves and *recommendations* of Congress : " That it be recommended to the
Legislatures of the several States to vest the United States, in
Congress assembled, (nine States to be represented in Congress and assenting) *for the term of fifteen years*, with power to
prohibit any goods, wares, and merchandizes, from being
imported into, or exported from any of the States, in vessels
belonging to, or navigated by, the subjects of any power
with whom these States shall not have formed treaties of
commerce ; and also with the power, during the same term,
of prohibiting the subjects of any foreign State, Kingdom,
or Empire, unless authorized by treaty, from importing into
the United States any goods, wares- or merchandize, which

are

which they probably intended, to hold up to the
eyes of Europe the appearance of their former
promptitude and vigour, while their apparent
energy concealed the moſt incurable irreſolution
and impotence. Like other limited powers the
Congreſs eaſily find an excuſe when they find themſelves unable to act. When they thought proper to
delay the forming of any arrangement of garriſons
for the weſtern and northern poſts they declared
in February laſt the reaſon to be ; that *nine States*
had been then only repreſented for a few days, nor
could it be conſidered till *the States became more
attentive to keeping up a full repreſentation in Congreſs* *.
When they are preſſed by the incapacity of paying
either the principal or intereſt of their debts, they
very coolly, but *truly*, avow †, that ſome of the States
have either refuſed, declined, or modified their recommendations for taxes. Experience ſince the
peace, were we to diſregard what happened during the war, ought to convince all reaſonable
men how impoſſible it is to procure the aſſent of
thirteen democratic aſſemblies, much leſs of four
and twenty ‡, to any meaſure which involves the
complicated intereſts of all: And the diſſent of

Y 2

one

are not the produce or manufacture of the dominions of the
Sovereign, whoſe ſubjects they are."—Such is the iſſue of
the Congreſs's pregnancy.

* Same Continental Journal.

† By the Budget 1784.

‡ Which number includes Vermont and the ten States,
that have been lately eſtabliſhed in the vaſt country, which
is bounded by the Ohio, the Miſſiſſippi, and the Lakes.

one State, like the *veto* of Poland, prevents effectually the fuccefs of the moft earneft recommendations; becaufe the powers given by the refpective affemblies are generally qualified with a provifo, *that the other affemblies likewife concur.* And while fome of the States lately impofed reftrictive duties on commerce, Connecticut and New Jerfey *opened free ports,* with a wifer purpofe and more certain benefit.

But, let us admit, that the Congrefs are already invefted with all the powers, which they have thus requefted of the Thirteen States, what character, we may afk, would they exhibit to the eyes of Europe: They would doubtlefs appear to Ruffia, who has refufed to enter into treaty with them, and to other powers, who have not yet thought it neceffary, or found it convenient, to form any commercial compacts, as a bully, who with a pen in one hand, and a fword in the other, declares : *You fhall treat, or you fhall not trade.* But, the coward alone fubmits to the uplifted cudgel : And the people, who allow their opponent to write the terms of peace, or of commerce, while the fword is brandifhed over the tablet, confefs to the world, that they are in the laft ftage of decline. To thofe however, who know the Congrefs the beft, that famous affembly, in the character, which they have thus chofen to affume for themfelves, will more likely refemble the boy, who was humoroufly exhibited by Reynolds, in the drefs and figure of Harry VIII. and who impreffed

preffed the mind with the idea of a perfonage of
great bulk with *little force.*

The agents of Congrefs fometimes act, as if they
thought the world were ignorant of their affairs,
and were unacquainted with their jurifprudence.
This truth we might even collect from thofe claufes
of the French and Dutch treaties, which ftipulate
feveral benefits in favour of the United States,
without other equivalent than the protection of
laws, which cannot be denied. The French however are now fully informed of their affairs, as we
may learn from the following anecdote. In order
to gain from Monf. De Vergennes an extenfion of
commerce, or additional privileges, the Congrefs
agents flattered lately, and fometimes foothed, and
at length bullied the great Minifter of a powerful
nation : Why, Gentlemen, faid Monf. de Vergennes peevifhly, you talk, as if you thought I
were unacquainted with your powers and with the
inability of your Congrefs to grant ampler one's ;
or as if I knew not, that the treaty, which I have
already made with you, will be no longer kept,
than the Congrefs ftand in need of his Majefty's
bounty, or than the individual States find an intereft in fulfilling it." Without the fagacity of
De Vergennes we may infer indeed, from the
terms of the confederation, that every affembly
poffeffes a referved right, to impofe as high cuftoms on foreigners, as fhall at any time be paid
by their own people, notwithftanding any treaty ;
and may prohibit the import, or reftrain their export,

of

of any goods, even contrary to the moſt ſolemn ſtipulations. So abſurd it is to attempt to modify the ſovereign power under a republican any more than under a monarchical form : So inconſiſtent is the exerciſe, or even exiſtence, of two ſovereign powers, much more *thirteen*, or *four and twenty* ſovereign powers, at one and the ſame time, within the ſame empire. While the Congreſs can neither impoſe taxes, nor regulate trade, they ought to be regarded as a body of men, with whom it is illuſory and idle to form a commercial treaty.

It is doubtleſs a queſtion of ſtill higher conſe-quence to inquire, whether the United States have faithfully executed the late Treaty of Peace, before we deliberately enter into any new one. It has been ſaid, by a profeſſed apologiſt of Congreſs indeed *; that the reſentment, which America felt againſt this country, during the war, ſubſided very un-expectedly at the peace, though it did not at that time againſt the American *Refugees* ; that ſtrong marks of a diſpoſition to relinquiſh their reſentments and ſettle in peace have already appeared : For, *many Refugees have been reſtored in different parts of Ame-rica :* And the Legiſlature of South Carolina paſſed an act in their laſt ſeſſion, which extends to *almoſt the whole number*—" for reſtoring certain perſons to their eſtates and permitting them to return to this State."——Happy for the preſent intereſts of the United States and for their future glory had this

extenuating

---

* Mr. Champion's Conſiderations on Commerce, p. 229·31.

extenuating reprefentation been as perfectly true as
it is extremely queftionable, in the moft effential
affirmations.

If the faithful performance of a folemn Treaty
is an object of any confequence to a great nation,
jealous of the honour of fovereignty, it muft be
furely of ufe to inquire minutely, how the American Treaty has been actually executed. The
Articles of Peace, which were concluded with
the United States, on the 30th of November 1782, were denominated *Provifional*, becaufe
it was agreed that they fhould not conftitute
a Treaty, till terms of peace, were agreed on
between Great Britain and France. When the
French Treaty was ere long fettled, the Articles
that had been thus Provifional, became at once
obligatory ; and formed confequently the rules of
conduct for the Contracting Powers. It was in
conformity to this reafoning, that the French Pre-
liminary Treaty was formally publifhed, when it
arrived at Philadelphia on the 24th of March 1783,
as the Provifional Articles had been announced to
the American world by Congrefs, twelve days before : It was in conformity to the foregoing reafoning, that the Congrefs proclaimed a ceffation of
arms on the 11th of April 1783; when hoftilities
immediately ceafed and prifoners were foon after-
difcharged. And the general pofition, That the
Provifional Articles bound the Congrefs from the
day on which they received them, and the citizens of
the United States from the moment thofe Articles
were

were made known to them, is conformable to the law of nations and is confirmed by the practicc of the civilized world." " A Treaty of Peace, fays Vattel, binds the contracting parties from the moment of its conclufion, unlefs it is otherwife ftipulated. When no term is affigned for the accomplifhment of the Treaty, common fenfe dictates, that every point fhould be executed as foon as poffible. And the faith of Treaties equally excludes from the execution of them all neglect, all dilatorinefs, aud all deliberate delays."

The recommendations, which had been ftipulated to be *earneftly made* by Congrefs : and which ought thus to have been iffued with all *convenient fpeed* ; were ftudioufly delayed notwithftanding the dictates of the law of nations and the requefts of the Britifh Commander of the American army *. The violences, which fucceeded the ceffation of arms, even prevented the evacuation of New-York, as had been ftipulated by Treaty. And the perfecution,

---

* Sir Guy Carleton wrote the Congrefs a letter, on the 17th of Auguft 1783 ; wherein he informed them, that he had received orders to evacuate New-York ; but, that the violence which had broke out immediately after the ceffation of arms had retarded that meafure : And he expreffed his concern, " That the Congrefs had thought proper to fufpend to this *late hour* the recommendations ftipulated by the Treaty, in the punctual performance of which the King and his Minifters have expreffed fuch entire confidence." The Congrefs never took any notice of this commendable letter ; becaufe it was impoffible to anfwer incontrovertible facts, whence ivevitable inferences had been drawn.

fecution, which enfued againſt the unfortunate
ſupporters of the Britiſh Government, ought to be
blotted from the page of hiſtory, were it not neceſſary for the inſtruction of mankind, to preſerve
examples of human depravity and of human fol-
lies, againſt the prevalence of which, the reaſon
and religion of men ought always to ſtruggle. Yet,
to determine with regard to the conduct of any
State, from the tumultuous irregularities of the
populace, who are eaſily agitated though not eaſily
calmed, would be as unfair as it would be undig-
nified. It is from authoritative acts alone that we
ought to form opinions of the proceedings, either
legal or illegal, of any Government. And it might
be minutely ſhewn, were it now either uſeful or
pleaſant, that every American State continued to
act authoritatively, from the 12th of March 1783,
when the Proviſional Articles were formally publiſhed, till the 14th of January 1784*, when the
Definitive Treaty was earneſtly recommended by
Congreſs, with regard to the unhappy objects of
thoſe recommendations, as if ſafety and reſtitution
had not been ſolemnly ſtipulated for them.

Z   Complete

* The packet from Falmouth conveyed the Definitive
Treaty to New York, on the 1ſt of November 1783. On
the 5th the Congreſs adjourned from Prince-town to Anna-
polis ; where Mr. Mifflin, the Preſident, arrived on the 3d of
December. Thaxter; the Secretary of Mr. Adams, brought
the Treaty on the 26th of November, which was publiſhed by
Congreſs on the 11th of December 1783. Dates are of great
importance, when we are inquiring with regard to the performance of Treaties.

Complete peace was furely eſtabliſhed on the 14th of January 1784, when the Congreſs ratified the Definitive Treaty, if it did not, in faſt, and in law, exiſt before *. And we may now pertinently aſk if the United States have honeſtly executed the ſolemn ſtipulations of a Treaty, from which they derived *as the valuable conſiderations of it*, peace, liberty and ſafety. From the annunciations of their own Gazettes we may learn indeed, that ſome of the States continued to expel thoſe objects of perſecution and neglect, who had a right given them by Treaty to ſolicit their affairs, as if they could not reſide as alien *friends*, under the municipal law of the Commonwealth; that all of thoſe Governments have continued to diſpoſe of the confiſcated property, which they had engaged to reſtore. And it may be added as a fact, as true as it will be memorable in their annals, that not one of the American Aſſemblies have complied with the recommendations of Congreſs—" To reſtore mens' rights and eſtates, as ſtipulated; to reviſe the acts of confiſcation, ſo as to make them confiſtent with the rules of juſtice, and the ſpirit of reconcilement."

The

---

* The Negotiators of Congreſs informed that body by their letter dated the 18th of July 1783, which was publiſhed in the Pennſylvania Independent Gazetteer of the 24th of April 1784: That the clauſe of the Treaty, which ſtipulates that there ſhall be no future confiſcations; ought to relate to the time of the ceſſation of arms; as the *Definitive Treaty ought to be conſidered, as only giving dreſs and form to the foregoing contracts and not as conſtituting the obligations of them.*

We fhall be enabled to judge of the truth of thofe broad pofitions, by a very fhort difcuffion. It is a peace-making principle of the law of nations, that every treaty of peace, without exprefs provifions, extinguifhes virtually all wrongs, which had been done during the previous war, fo that they fhall not be deemed caufes of future difpute. Yet, the American Legiflatures * feem all to have directed, fince the re-eftablifhment of amity, that accounts fhall be taken of devaftations committed by the Britifh army, during the courfe of feven years hoftilities. With whatever view this Legiflative direction was given, the principle whence it proceeded, is undoubtedly hoftile. And it was cautious, though unneceffary in our negotiators to ftipulate exprefsly by treaty, that no profecutions fhall be commenced in future againft perfons, for the part they had taken in the war, or on that account fuffer any future damage. Yet, the government of New-York have empowered their citizens by a law, denominated in their jurifprudence, *the trefpafs act*, to fue any perfons for injuries done to property, during the war, and to fubject any one who fhall have refided, while the Britifh army garrifoned New-York, in any houfe only for a day to the rent for feven years. This in the energetic

Z 2   language

---

* Virginia act October 1783, ch. 10. " For continuing an act to afcertain the loffes and injuries fuftained from the depredations of the enemy within this State." The peaceful Pennfylvania took the lead of this hoftile meafure. And Carolina, Georgia, and others followed the example of both.

language of Phocion*, was *to enact a civil war*: And some persons have actually been imprisoned, under its authority, and others have been obliged to flee. With a similar spirit the government of South Carolina set aside, since the peace, the decisions of the Court of Police, which had been erected, while Charles Town was occupied by British troops; and British subjects who had purchased property under its decisions or had appealed to its equity, have been condemned in damages, and have been either imprisoned, or forced to abandon their families and affairs; though by the laws of war the conquest of the country carries with it the peaceful right of governing the people, by proper judicatories.

Nevertheless we are boastingly told, " That the Legislature of South Carolina in their last session passed an act for restoring the estates of *almost the whole number* of attainted persons†." But, Mr. Champion either did not know, or at least did not tell the whole truth. Certain indeed it is, that the assembly passed an act, in pursuance of the recommendation of Congress, and the requests of the Governor, for restoring out of about six hundred

confiscated

---

* The title of two able defences of the treaty, which have been published, in opposition to the spirit of the times, by the late Secretary of General Washington, Colonel Hamilton; a gentleman, whose pen is as powerful as his sword.

† Mr. Champion's Considerations.—The Jacksonborough act of 1782, attainted about two hundred persons by name and upwards of four hundred more by description.

confifcated eftates, one hundred and twenty-four, on fpecific conditions. Yet, let us attend to two only of thofe effential ones: 1ftly, It is directed by the act as a *previous* condition, " That the parties, their attornies or agents fhould make a true return upon oath of their eftates, real and perfonal, in order that the commiffioners fhould caufe an affeffment of twelve *per cent.* on the real value of fuch eftates to be paid *in fpecie*, before the firft day of March then next, with an addition of two *per cent.* to the Commiffioners of Confifcation: 2dly, The law gave an option to the purchafers of confifcated property to relinquifh or retain it, and in this laft cafe the owner is only allowed to receive in fatisfaction the fecurities, that had been given in payment by buyers, or *indents*, a fpecies of paper money, which, with the ufual fate of American paper, had already depreciated four-fifths of its original value. In this manner were the parties obliged to pay before the firft of March fourteen in the hundred of the genuine value of their eftates in *real* money ; yet to receive in fatisfaction *fictitious* money at a future day. And in this manner did the Affembly of South Carolina fulfil * the treaty and

regard

---

* That there was no real purpofe to execute the treaty, or to comply with the Congrefs, may be indeed inferred, from the public notice, which the Commiffioners gave in April laft, purfuant to an ordinance of Affembly, dated the 26th of March, 1784, for amending and explaining the confifcation act. The State Gazette gave notice " to all purchafers of

confifcated

regard the recommendations of Congrefs, which admited not of partial modifications, fince all had been agreed to be reftored. Well may the perfons, who were merely reftored to their ruin, exclaim :

> And be thefe juggling fiends no more believed,
> That palter with us in a double fenfe,
> That keep the word of promife to our ear,
> And break it to our hope.

Yet, are we affured *, " that fuch an example, in a State, which has fuffered fo greatly by the war, affords the ftrongeft hope, that it will be followed in all the States." Yes ; Maffachufetts has in a great meafure followed the example of South Carolina, " *by making diftinctions of a fimilar* nature." The affembly of March 1784, recited †, 1ftly; " That whereas by the the fixth article of the treaty made between the United States and Great-Britain it is provided, that no further confifcations fhall be made :" It therefore enacted 2dly; that the lands which any of the perfons aforementioned held in fee fimple, or by a leffer eftate, on the 19th day of April 1775, and *have not* by the act entitled " An act to confifcate the eftates of certain notorious

confifcated property, where titles have *not been already made,* to apply for fuch titles and give the neceffary fecurity, on or before the 26th day of May next, (1784,) otherwife fuch property *will again be fold at public fale,* and the former purchafers made liable to all expences."

* By Mr. Champion's Confiderations.

† The act was publifhed in the Bofton Independent Chronicle of the 1ft of April, 1784.

rious conspirators against the government and liberties of the inhabitants of the late province, now
State of Massachusett's-Bay;" or by judgment had
on due process of law on such estates been confiscated, nor have been pledged by government for
money borrowed, or sold by Agents according to
the laws of the State for the payment of debts, due
from absentees, or have been made liable to pay
any annual charge for the support of any poor person; shall be delivered up to the parties, who
respectively owned such lands last before the 19th
of April 1775; or to any person claiming under
them respectively; provided such claimants are
not included in the act aforesaid, made in the
year 1778, who shall have the privilege of dispos-
ing of the same within the space of three years."
The words of the law were given, to enable every
one to judge for himself. A large body of men,
" who were deemed to hold principles and possess
dispositions incompatible with the safety of the
Commonwealth," were by the same law excluded
from returning to Massachusett's: A less obnoxious
class was allowed to reside upon obtaining a licence
from the Governor, which was to continue no
longer in force than the meeting of the next
assembly.

Yet, the treaty stipulated, for the restitution of
all confiscated rights; for the admission of all those
who had borne arms against the States, to solicit
restitution; for a revision of such acts as prevented
reconcilement: The treaty expressly provided, that
there

there shall be no future confiscations ; that no perfon
fhall fuffer future damage for the part which he
acted during the war. It was furely a commendable rule of the old-fafhioned writers on the law of
nations, that plain words fhall be conftrued according to their ufual import and juft agreements fhall
be executed according to the obvious meaning of
the Contracting Powers. But, to exclude men, who
ought to be admitted ; to deny reftitution of thofe
rights, which were to be reftored to former owners ;
and to add additional penalties to laws, which were
to be made more confiftent with juftice ; all thefe
are the novel conftructions, which our fafhionable
Philofophers recommend to be given to our
American treaty. *Confifcation*, fays Bacon, *is the
act of transferring the forfeited goods of criminals to public ufe.* The Legiflative declaration then prefcribed
merely the mode : The fale of the confifcated property and the application of the price to the fervice of the State formed the real transfer of the
goods to the public ufe, much more than the law.
To provide by treaty, that no additional modes
fhould be enacted, at an epoch, when there remained no perfons, or things, whereon future
laws could work, was furely no reafonable act. The
exprefs ftipulation, that there fhould be no future
confifcation ought to be therefore conftrued, fince
it was certainly meant, to fignify no future appro-
priation of the forfeited property ; and every de-
tention ought to be deemed a new transfer of the
                                                  things

things to be reftored from the obnoxious individual to the more delinquent ftate.——But, it is
now faid, that the making of the diftinctions among
perfons to be reftored, where the treaty makes
none; the deducting of amercements from property, in cafes where the treaty infifts, that the
party fhall fuffer no future damage; and the declaring by law a body of men to be enemies to a
government, while by the treaty they are admitted
to be friends; all thefe topics are fuggefted rather
than faid to be ftrong marks of a defire in the
American citizens to allow their refentments to
fubfide. He who in this apologetical fpirit infifts,
that the performance of part of the American
treaty is the fulfilment of all, muft allow us to
argue that, by the fame rule of inference, the
greateft is lefs than the leaft; that by this new-
fangled logick, the performance of no part what-
foever is more confiftent with the good faith wherewith treaties ought to be performed, than the literal
execution of the minuteft ftipulation. But, in vain
does reafon contend with the gripe of avarice or
with the obduracy of power. And who can fupprefs
indignation, when he fees experience infulted by
puerility, or reftrain ridicule, when he feels common fenfe fhocked by the fooleries of Philofophy.

If candour is as commendable as a virtue, as
chicanery is defpicable as a vice, the avowed conduct of New-York muft be much more approved,
than the pretended compliance of South Carolina
and Maffachufett's, or even than the contemptuous

filence

silence of other States. They have all refused virtually: But, to deny bluntly is at least more manly than to feign a fulfilment, which is not meant.—— After two months consideration, the New-York assembly resolved, on the 30th of March, 1784: " That, as on the one hand, the rules of Justice do not require, so on the other hand the public tranquility will not admit, that such adherents, who have been attainted should be restored to the rights of citizenship and there can be no reason for restoring property, which has been confiscated, *as no compensation is offered on the part of Great-Britain, for the damages sustained by this State from the devastations of the war:* And that, while the legislature entertain the highest sense of national honour and the sanction of treaties and of the deference, which is due to the advice of the United States in Congress, they find it inconsistent with their duty to comply with the recommendation of the said United States, on the subject of the 5th article of the Definitive Treaty: Therefore resolved by both houses, that the Governor be desired to transmit these resolutions to Congress." This is a language, which cannot be made plainer by commentaries.

While this intemperate spirit reigns in the American legislatures, we are told by their apologist, *that many refugees have been restored in different parts of America.* We may, for the convenience of argument, grant to Mr. Champion the truth of his position, though the fact is unfounded, as it was meant to be exhibited to the public, and then beg

to

to know, what he would infer from it. That certain perfons, (and fewer there were, who difgraced themfelves by their neutrality, during the late civil broils, than had ever exifted in fimilar contefts before) who, being fhocked at the fight of rebellion, or war, fought refuge in happier climes. It is admitted, that fome of thofe perfons may have been reftored to fome of their rights, becaufe, having been moved by confiderations of age, of fex, or infirmities, they had committed no greater crime againft the Commonwealths, than that of deferting them, when danger approached.————— But, thofe are not the men, who were prompted, by their fpirit, to face tumult and bloodfhed; and were engaged, by their loyalty, to rifque their perfons and property, and to draw their fwords, in fupport of the rights of Britain. And thefe are the men, whom we have feen expelled, and excluded, and deftroyed, by every mode of perfecution *.

The mind is naturally led to compare times, either happy, or difaftrous, which feem nearly alike in their political features, King William had fcarcely atchieved the Revolution, when the

A a 2   perfecuted

---

* Several of thofe loyal perfons, who have returned to the United States, fince the peace, were arrefted by creditors, who may have taken different fides, though their property and credits had been taken away by the State. Other loyal perfons, who remain in Britain, are fued by the American creditors here, though the confifcated effects had been appropriated to the payment of American debts, and they are difqualified from fuing their debtors in the American courts. Thus, are the Loyalifts thrown into the bed of Procruftes.

perfecuted proteftants of France looked for fhelter in England, in confiderable numbers, and found it. In the fate of unhappy ftrangers, who ran thus under the wings of England, the Parliament interefted themfelves, and thereby gained for England the celebration of the world, by bountifully fupplying their needs, amid greater embarraffments of war, and finance, than have occurred at any time fince *. The Irifh nobility and gentry, who, becaufe they were attached to England and fupported the Revolution, were attainted by the Irifh Parliament of the abdicated monarch, equally fought protection at that æra from England, which was ftill more amply given by Parliament, fince their claims were ftronger †. Thofe Parliamentary precedents clearly evince the great diverfity there is, between Mr. Champion's *refugees* and thofe *faithful American fubjects*, whom every Englifhman ought to regard, if it is meritorious to have fupported the rights of England, by their talents, their property, and arms: The French refugees afked and received the charity of the nation: The Irifh loyalifts claimed of the juftice of Parliament, and from its equity received, not only immediate affiftance but ultimate compenfation.

But,

* There were 3,500 French refugees, to whom were given £.15,000 a year, during the reign of William. [Com. Journal, 10 v. p. 116. Hift. of Debts, part ii. p. 1.]

† Com. Journal, 10 v. p. 204—12—217—29. Vol. 13, p. 291—3. Vol. 15, p. 36—48—68—344.

But, the claim of the American Loyalifts feems to be a ftronger one. Their natural inclination was ftrengthened by the Parliamentary refolutions of 1766 *. Their ardour was incited by the Secretary of State's private inftructions ; whereby Governors were exhorted, *to offer every encouragement to thofe, who appeared in principle adverfe,* to the proceedings of the malcontents. Their apprehenfions amid dangers were removed, by the Royal proclamation of Auguft 1775 ; which gave affurances, " *that none* ought to *doubt the protection, which the law will afford to their loyalty and zeal.*" And after all thefe previous incitements they were called forth into action, by the manifefto of the Royal Commiffioners, in June 1776 ; which declared, " That due confideration fhall be had to the meritorious fervices of all perfons, who fhall affift in reftoring the public tranquility and that *every fuitable encouragement fhall be given to thofe who fhall promote the re-eftablifhment of legal government.*" And in this manner was the faith of the King and Parliament pledged, and the pride of the people engaged in the face of the world, to grant honeft recompence to American *loyalifts,* though not to American *refugees,* as foon as—" diligent and impartial enquiry"—fhall have eftablifhed the truth of each particular claim.

Yet, it is added by the Apologift of Congrefs, " That though refentments did not immediately
fink

* Com. Journ. 30 vol. page 603. Wherein we may fee the Commons refolve : " *That thofe loyal fubjects, who had affifted in carrying the Acts of Parliament into execution, are entitled to the protection and favour of that Houfe.*"

sink towards the refugees, it did towards this country." ´ Candour ought frankly to confess, That it was to have been expected of men, who had given mutual wounds and received mutual injuries, that they would not soon forgive or forget one another. And from this active principle of human nature wise men early inferred, what experience seems to have proved, that the treaty, in respect to the recovery of confiscations, would never be executed. Governments, at least ancient ones, have learned to suppress passion, which would disable them from discharging those essential duties, the restraining of the resentments of individuals, and the granting of universal right. In this considerate spirit Great Britain has acted since the epoch of independence, with respect to the United States. What returns the American Governments have made in those cooler cases, wherein their sense of injury did not lead their Legislatures astray, it is now proper to ask.

The treaty of peace (as we all know) expressly stipulated, *that there should be no lawful impediment to the recovery of Debts, on either side.* It required, as it is said, no small address and perseverance to procure this salutary stipulation from a people, who have never been famous for facilitating payment of debts. And the time is now come, when we ought to inquire how they have performed it. In Georgia, the Chief Justice, with his associates, determined (as hath been already evinced) that a British Merchant, being an alien *friend,* could not maintain

an

an action for debt, though they had pronounced, with the fame breath, *that the laws of England had been ftudded into the Georgian fyftem.* The South Carolina Affembly with a bolder fpirit paffed an act, on the 16th of March 1784 ; for preventing the commencement of fuits for debts contracted by any citizen previous to February 1782; and for poftponing ultimate payment by feveral liquidations till January 1789. Urged perhaps by the fame neceffities the North Carolina Affembly paffed an act, in May 1783, to prevent the recovery of debts theretofore contracted, till after the expiration of a year. Equally neceffitous, but perhaps more confident, the Virginian Affembly paffed an act, even after they had received the Definitive Treaty, " to fufpend the iffuing of executions for four months from December 1783, and to the end of the fubfequent Affembly. The American Legiflatures, who may have concurred with thofe States, in fimilar meafures, may equally plead, *that the neceffity which drives, defends.* Whether Grotius or Puffendorf, Burlamaqui or Vattel, would have admitted this juftification, for an evident infraction of a pofitive treaty is a queftion, which it is not at prefent worth while to afk. Their own Phocion has told the American citizens, with a loud voice, on the authority of fome of thofe jurifts : " That the wilful breach of a fingle article annuls the whole, fince every claufe muft ftand, or fall together. If Britain fhould regard the treaty as broken,—can we renew the war? We know ; and

all

all the world knows, it is out of our power. There
is a certain evil attends our intemperance, namely,
a loſs of character in Europe: For our Miniſters
write, that our conduct hitherto, in this reſpect,
has done us infinite injury; and has exhibited us in
the light of a people, deſtitute of government, on
whoſe engagements of courſe no dependence can
be placed."

We have been thus led round a circle of large
circumference, in order to come at the general
reſult, which has been in this manner drawn by
Phocion. And it muſt now be admitted, that
there ought to be a ſtrong neceſſity, or a very
apparent uſe, to juſtify the meaſure, of entering
into a new treaty with States, who have not,
even by their own acknowledgments, performed
the old. Of the exiſtence of that neceſſity, or of
that uſe it may be proper to make a few remarks.
The ſtipulation, which expreſsly promiſed, that
there ſhould be no lawful impediment to the recovery of debts, has been attended, as we have ſeen,
with no great efficacy, in the practice of merchants. Wiſe men, who had ſeen, during every
age, the ſame neceſſities prevailing in the Colonies,
whoſe Legiſlatures oppoſed ſimilar obſtructions to
the recovery of debts, have been heard to obſerve:
That the only point of commercial policy, which
had the ſemblance of uſe, would be an effectual
proviſion for the ſpeedy liquidation of debts, which
muſt always be due from the United States to Britain. And doubtleſs a ſtipulation of this kind (if

we

we had any security for its performance) would be
of great importance to a commercial people, who
seem to set no bounds to the number, or length of
the credits, which they have always given to too
distant customers. In confirmation of that remark
they have mentioned, as the greatest infelicity,
which perhaps has resulted to Britain from the
independence of her colonies, that it had virtually
repealed the statute *; which had enabled British
merchants to prove their debts before any Mayor
of any corporation, and subjected all property to
the payment of all debts.

The observation is in some measure just: But
the inference cannot be admitted in all its extent.
It has been established as a foundation, whereon
much may be built, that the United States had
wisely established it as a rule for the government of
their courts of justice, *to regard all laws of England
theretofore used and approved, as still in full force.* But,
the statute of George II. before mentioned had
been long used and approved. And unless the
judges, in the absurd spirit of Walton, the Georgian
Chief-justice, do violence to their own system, that
law must be allowed in every tribunal; not from the
vigour of the British Legislature, but from the
wisdom of their own adoption. The establishment
of this inference, however, and the introduction of
a convenient practice under it, must ultimately
depend on the temper of the Judges and the appro-

B b   bation

* 5 Geo. II. ch. 7.

bation of the people. And the American lawyers before they approve, or reject, a construction, which must prove beneficial to both countries, would do well to remember, that the Courts of Westminster-hall have been lately empowered, by the Legislature, to facilitate the suitors and to give scope to justice, by sending commissions to every corner of the earth, to examine evidences and to procure proofs. Great Britain and the United States from their mutual dealings are equally interested in this great improvement of juridical forms, because it may often be equally convenient to bring testimony from America to Britain *. And thus may the apprehensions of merchants be calmed on the interesting subject, how their American debts are now to be ascertained.

* There is reason to believe, that the American citizens rely more on the justice, speedy and impartial, of Westminster-hall, than on that of their own tribunals. In this spirit they have lately adopted a practice, which leads to unforseen consequences ; and which, were they foreseen, could not easily be prevented, however inconvenient they might be. The American citizens when they see any fellow-citizen is about to sail for Britain for the purpose of business rather than of settlement, and who may be indebted to them, allow the debtor to depart and arrest him upon his arrival in London. In this unexampled proceeding they have two views : 1stly, They rely on the singular justice of the country ; 2dly, They know, that their debtor carries with him a large sum of money with design to purchase a considerable cargo on the credit of what he pays down; and they hope by arresting their debtor on 'Change to intercept the money, and thereby procure speedier payment, than if they had stoped him in the American port. Such are the varieties of human affairs.

Were an intelligent perfon defired to fketch a Commercial Treaty with the United States, having fome regard to the foregoing confiderations, he would probably find himfelf extremely perplexed to difcover or to create ftipulations, which lead to any ufe, or which are dictated by any neceffity. He would do well firft to reflect, that it is fome neceffity or fome ufefulnefs, which ought to form the bafis of all commercial treaties : That every nation, having a right to judge of that ufefulnefs and of that neceffity, may approve or reject the equivalents, which had been offered for requefted immunities, without giving caufe of offence, or reafon for explanation. That to eftablifh again by Treaty what had been already eftablifhed by law is no reafonable act ; any more than it would be a wife meafure to make a new act of Parliament in a cafe where an old one already exifted ; which, ab-ftracted from its legiflative indecency, always creates doubts and introduces difficulties, that never exifted before. Were fuch a perfon afraid of the ridicule, which generally attends thofe, who gravely propofe to do that which has been already done, he would probably be induced by his fears, however he might be governed by his prudence, to confider, whether the laws have not more amply provided for the eafe and freedom of the American trade, than the Treaties, which the United States have concluded with Holland and France. And when he turned his attention to the actual ftate of the commerce between Great Britain and the

United

United States, as it has been lately regulated, on liberal principles, he would perhaps difcover little to amend, and confequently little to propofe, as the foundation of a fupplemental treaty.

The truth of the foregoing fuggeftions we fhall fee in a ftill more fatisfactory light, by flightly reviewing; 1ftly, Our export trade to the United States; 2dly, The nature of our imports from them; 3dly, The policy of the Weft-India regulations of our navigation.

1. The trade, which was already free has been made more free, by repealing * the ftatute of the prefent reign, that retained what was technically called *The Old Subfidy* on merchandize, which fhould be fent to the Britifh Colonies: And thereby the American citizens have actually gained, by this additional boon, what is certainly faved, about five in the hundred on the value of every cargo; and confequently £.150,000 a year, if the amount of their whole cargoes be £.3,000,000. This meafure forms a fingular inftance of our legiflative liberality and evinces our encreafing knowledge of the nature of trade, from the filent efforts of truth.

2. He

* The 30th of July 1784, will be remarkable in our commercial annals, for the paffing of an act of Parliament—" To difcontinue the petty cuftom on aliens goods imported into Great Britain and the duty of one *per cent.* on goods exported to, or imported from the Mediterranean Seas in unqualified fhips; and for repealing fo much of an act, paffed in the fourth year of his prefent Majefty, as enacts, that no part of the Old Subfidy fhall be drawn back upon any goods exported to the Britifh Plantations in America."

2. He to whom fhall be affigned the difficult tafk of making a Commercial Treaty with the United States will find his chief embarraffments to arife from the regulation of the exports from that country to Britain. He will fee they have been already allowed the free importation of all their *unmanufactured* products, which includes almoft all their furplufes, on paying the fame duties as are paid on fuch commodities when brought in from the Britifh Plantations. Their naval ftores and their lumber are thus exempted from duties; And they are allowed the fole fupply of tobacco on terms of the greateft facility. But, the United States, it feems are not content: They defire to fend all their commodities to Britain, the productions of their fifhery as well as the produce of their agriculture; fince they lay no reftraint on the importation of Britifh manufactures, which thus, they argue, find a prodigious vent. Yet, both parties will do well to remember, that it is mutual convenience more than fancied reciprocity, which ought to form the bafis of all commercial treaties. Our fuppofed Negotiator may be thence led to inquire how fuch a propofal, were it carried into effect, would affect our induftrious claffes, who all merit protection, but fome of them particular favour. Such of them as contribute to our defence in war deferve greater attention from the State than thofe, who augment our opulence in peace. Whence, we ought to rank our induftrious people in the following order of merit: The failors are

the

the men who deferve moft of our care, becaufe they
are the great protectors of every other clafs, in the
enjoyment of their freedom from the attacks of the
foe. The next in order and fecond in merit are
our fhipwrights and joiners, and other artificers,
connected with the outfit of fhips, becaufe they are
the builders of our *wooden walls*, and without them
even the gallant efforts of the failors are vain.
The farmers ftand third in rank, if not the firft,
becaufe they furnifh every other clafs with food.
And the workers in wool, whofe peculiar interefts
have been too often preferred to the general good,
can only be ranked in the fourth place. If convenience then be the rule of difapprobation, or affent,
in forming treaties of commerce, it can never be
right to admit the oil and fifh of New England,
becaufe her citizens confume many of the manufactures of wool, fince this meafure would facrifice
the intereft of the two moft meritorious claffes to
the gratification of the fourth. But, let us for the
accommodation of argument fuppofe, that the New
Englanders offered to difregard their agreements
with Holland and France, and to admit *exclufively*
the woollen manufactures of Britain, and let us
then afk, would fuch a monopoly be for the real
intereft of Britain, were it truly carried into effect.
We fhall beft anfwer this interefting queftion, by
afking feveral other queftions. Does not the hiftory
of wool in this Ifland evince, that the manufacturers
of wool, have too often tyrannized over every other
clafs and even dictated to the Legiflature; that they

have

'have often difturbed the public repofe by their clamours and fometimes broken the public peace by
their tumults ? Did not thofe diforders proceed
from the previous impolicy, of vefting too much
capital in one branch of bufinefs and employing too
many hands in one kind of manufacture ; whereby
the fame evil was introduced into the community,
as if a wen were on purpofe created on the body
natural, which might begin with mortification and
end with death. In this view of the fubject would
it be for the real advantage of Britain, were the
world to give her the *exclufive privilege* of fupplying
the world with the fabricks of wool ? was it not
prudent in the Legiflature to encourage the weavers
of filk, of cotton, and linnen, as competitors to
the weavers of wool, with the wife defign to
draw gradually hands from a fuperabundant clafs to
employments of a fomewhat different kind, whofe
fewnefs of numbers from the want of occupation,
did not lead to groundlefs alarm and even to
dangerous tumult. May we not thence infer it
to be the duty of wife Legiflators to keep up continually an exact balance among the induftrious
claffes of a commercial and naval nation, fo that
none of them fhall have too many hands or
any of them too few. Would not the New-England propofal counteract this falutary policy and
neceffarily tend to introduce an evil rather than a
good ? And thus have we difcuffed in a paragraph
a difficult fubject of political œconomy, which
ought indeed to occupy a volume.

3. But

3. But however free and advantageous the commerce may be between Great Britain and the United States, the rights of trade between the two mother countries gives no pretence for traffic with Colonies, if we may rely on the weighty decision of Montefquieu, or the ftill weightier dictates of common fenfe. Like the fyftem of other European powers the laws of Great Britain forbade all foreigners to trade with our tranfatlantic fettlements: Our Government relaxed the rigour of thofe laws, in kindnefs to our Colonies and favour to the United States. Yet, the proclamation of the 2d of July 1783, is faid *to have come upon both as a thunderclap.* And the moment of furprife had no fooner paffed away with the cloud, than modes of circumvention and even meafures of recal were purfued with the ardour of men, who are urged at once by faction and intereft. The arts which had produced the Colonial revolt were naturally adopted. And inftigatory letters were written to the United States as well as to the Weft Indies, to join in concerted clamour and to adopt various meafures to gain their different ends. But, intrigues, which are detected and known, are no longer dangerous. And the admiffion of the American veffels into the Weft India ports muft be gained by treaty, fince the force of threats have failed. It is now time to afk what are the equivalents which they offer for the boon that they beg ; as in every operation of commerce fomething muft be given for fomething. The United States have precluded themfelves, by

treaty

treaty from granting to Britain any peculiar facility in trade. It has been fuggefted rather than fhewn that the grant of any exclufive fupply of any of the manufactures of Britain would be hurtful rather than beneficial to her genuine interefts; would be an evil rather than a good. But, we offer you large markets for your manufactures, fay the United States: We give you large credits, fays Britain; we furnifh you with capital, in proportion to the debts you detain; and we open moreover an extenfive market for all your unmanufactured products. Are we not cuftomers to your tradefmen to the annual amount of three million, nay of fix million, of fterling pounds, fubjoin the United States: The queftion is not, Britain replies, whether you are a *great* cuftomer, but whethe you are a *good* one: Our warehoufemen have fenfe enough to know, that they grow rich by fupplying not *one great* cuftomer, but *many fmall* one's: Our Statefmen fee clearly enough, that neither the intereft nor fafety of the nation can ever confift in trafficing with any one community to fo vaft an extent, that any accidental failure, or purpofed non-importation, would occafion outcries and convulfions; whereby one of the greateft of nations might be fubjected difgracefully to her cuftomers and debtors.

It muft afford confolation to every honeft mind to be fhewn, that, in the prefent ftate of American trade, it is plainly impoffible for the United States to take any legiflative ftep, without promoting the

C c   commercial

commercial intereft of Britain. Were they to
ftop the whole of their exports to the Britifh Weft-
Indies, they would thereby give a bounty to
Canada, Nova Scotia, and Newfoundland; and
they would by that means force Britain into that
fyftem of fupply and navigation, which fhe is prevented from adopting fpontaneoufly, by the prejudices of the many, rather than by the reafonings
of the few. Were the United States to impofe
taxes on the import of Britifh manufactures this
ftep would equally lead to the real advantage of
Britain : If the taxed articles fhould be neceffaries
the American confumer would pay the duty : If they
fhould be only luxuries, which the American citizen
would do well not to confume, Britain ought not
to fend the goods that could not be fpeedily paid
for. If the Congrefs fhould be even enabled to
go the full length of enacting, *that the State, which
will not treat, fhall not trade*, the intereft of Britain
would equally be promoted : For, to the amount
of the neceffaries, the merchants of Britain would
continue to fend, as they fent them during the
war, by Flanders, by Holland, by France ; whofe
wealthier and more punctual traders would become
our paymafters, who are more under our eye :
And to tranfmit the United States greater cargoes
than they can poffibly pay for cannot be eafily
juftified. By prudent perfeverance, in meafures
moderate and juft, much has already been gained.
To derive every poffible advantage from the American

rican trade nothing more is wanting, than for the nation to be quiet and the Parliament to fit ftill.

Such are the opinions, which the author of the foregoing fheets has prefumed, perhaps impru-dently, to avow to the world. Amid the anxieties, which moft men feel, in fpeaking truths to a world, that is not always confiderate and kind, he has fome confolations. If his opinions fhall be deemed weak one's, they may be eafily confuted, or ftill more eafily neglected. If they fhall be regarded as weighty ones, he will have the fatisfaction of reflecting, that he has contributed his drops to the ftream of truth, which as it runs filently and un-heeded by, leaves the improvements, refulting from intelligence, in the country behind. The documents, which his diligence has gleaned, will remain, when the hand that collected them fhall be cold; and the reflections, which he has anxioufly made, may perhaps caufe a few others to think, when the head and the heart, that formed the re-fult, have been long laid low in the duft.

F I N I S.

** The reader is defired to correct the following errors, which affect the fenfe :

In page 11—faid for fad.
76—440 for 4,040.
86—land Mary for Maryland.
92—abetting for abating.

BOOKS printed for J. DEBRETT,
oppofite Burlington-Houfe, Piccadilly.

This Day is Publifhed, Price 2s.

THE PARLIAMENTARY REGISTER, Numbers XIV. and XV. of the laft Seffion of Parliament, and XCIV. and XCV. from the General Election in 1780.

The PARLIAMENTARY REGISTER, from the General Election in 1774, to the Diffolution in 1780, in feventeen volumes, price 6l. 6s.

The Firft, Second, and Third Seffions of the laft Parliament, in eleven volumes, price 4l. 7s. half bound and lettered.

The thirteen preceding Numbers of the laft Seffion, price 1s. each.

⁎ Thofe Gentlemen wno want any particular Numbers to complete their Sets, are earneftly defired to order them as fpeedily as poffible.

☞ The Editors beg leave to return their warmeft thanks to thofe Noblemen and Gentlemen, by whofe diftinguifhed patronage and aid they have been able to conduct Publication through the two laft Parliaments, in a manner that hath entitled the Work to the approbation of the Public. The communications with which they have been honoured, have been attended to with the utmoft care, and upon every queftion the ftricteft candour has been obferved, that the Work might contain a true and faithful account of every important Debate.

The ELEVENTH REPORT from the Select Committee, appointed to take into confideration the State of the Adminiftration of Juftice in the Provinces of Bengal, Bahar, and Oriffa. Price 2s.

⁎ This Report contains an account of money received and acknowledged by the Hon. Warren Haftings, Governor General of Bengal.

A REPLY to Mr. BURKE's SPEECH on the firft of December, 1783. By Major JOHN SCOTT, Price 1s. 6d.

The REMEMBRANCER; or IMPARTIAL REPOSITORY of PUBLIC EVENTS. Price 1s. each Number.—The American war gave rife to this Work in 1775. Every authentic paper relative to that war, as alfo with France and Spain, whether publifhed in England or America, by the Britifh Miniftry or the American Congrefs, are all carefully inferted in this work. The letters of the feveral commanding officers, addreffes, refolutions of the various committees, conventions, &c. Complete fets of this valuable and interefting work may be had of the publifher in feventeen volumes. Price Six Guineas, half-bound and lettered.